THE MAKING OF A BEAUTIFUL VESSEL

THE MAKING OF A BEAUTIFUL VESSEL

Predestined for Purpose

IRIS DUPREE-WILKES

authorHOUSE®

AuthorHouse™
1663 Liberty Drive
Bloomington, IN 47403
www.authorhouse.com
Phone: 1-800-839-8640

Published by AuthorHouse   02/21/2013

ISBN: 978-1-4817-0640-7 (sc)
ISBN: 978-1-4817-0639-1 (e)

Unless otherwise indicated, Scripture is taken from the New King James Version Copyright 1979, 1980, 1982 by Thomas Nelson, Inc.

Scripture marked NIV is taken from the HOLY BIBLE, NEW INTERNATIONAL VERSION, Copyright 1973, 1978, 1984 International Bible Society. Used by permission of Zondervan Publishing House. All rights reserved.

Scripture marked AMP is taken from Internet Web site: www.biblegateway.com, AMPLIFIED, Copyright 1995-2010, The Zondervan Corporation.

Scripture marked NLT is taken from Internet Web site: www.biblegateway.com, NEW LIVING TRANSLATION, Copyright 1995-2010, The Zondervan Corporation.

Scripture marked CEB is taken from Internet Web site: www.biblegateway.com, COMMON ENGLISH BIBLE, Copyright 1995-2010, The Zondervan Corporation.

Scripture marked MSG is taken from Internet Web site: www.biblegateway.com, MESSAGE BIBLE, Copyright 1995-2010, The Zondervan Corporation.

All definitions taken from:
Webster II New Riverside University Dictionary, Copyright 1984, 1988; by Houghton Mifflin Company

Quotes:
Mr. Charles E. Lewis, Sr., D. Min.

CONTENTS

The Making of A Beautiful Vessel

"[20] But in a great house there are not only vessels of gold and silver, but also of wood and clay, some for honor and some for dishonor. [21] Therefore if anyone cleanses himself from the latter; he will be a vessel for honor, sanctified and useful for the Master, prepared for every good work" (2 Timothy 2:20-21, NKJV).

Predestined for Purpose

When God created life in the Garden of Eden it was beautiful. Your life is a beautiful gift, it's a privilege and it's predestined for purpose. Who can agree with me that the most beautiful things in life experience testing and trials? Have your testing and trials caused you to feel stuck, living in captivity? Are you struggling in life? Do you feel inadequate? If so, you need to understand Satan's goal is to destroy you. He tries to deceive you into thinking your life is as good as it will ever get. This is a lie because Satan is the father of lies; he hates the truth, and therefore, uses different tactics to make you feel inadequate and stuck so you can give up on life all together. Are you a vessel for honor or dishonor? Are you useful for the Master, prepared for every good work? Sons and daughters of the King remember you are blessed and God has so much more for you. In the midst of your testing and trials learn to enjoy life, stop allowing yourself to be held in captivity being controlled by the devil. *"[22-24] Run away from infantile indulgence. Run after mature righteousness—faith, love, peace—joining those who are in honest and serious prayer before God. Refuse to get involved in inane discussions; they always end up in fights. God's servant must not be argumentative, but a gentle listener and a teacher who keeps cool . . ." (2 Timothy 2:22-24, MSG).* We must learn to stay focused on the purposes of God for our life.

This book will encourage you to keep building your life, no matter what you are facing. As you continue reading this book, we will journey through the path of your life and you shall be set free so that you can move forward in Christ and display that beautiful vessel that God has called you to be.

Acknowledgements

To my Husband and Children:

Michael Wilkes, my husband of 17 years, and to my witty and charming children; Omar and Alexis thank you so much for all of your love, support, and understanding. I pray that each of you will fulfill the call that God has on your life. I love you!

To my Parents:

Connie (deceased) and Olivia Dupree the best parents in the world, thank you for all your love and support you have given throughout the years. I thank God for our family unity. I love you!

To my Brothers and Sister:

Mark, Fred, Gwen, and Blaney; thank you for everything I love you guys and I appreciate all the special moments we've had together. I pray God's choice blessings upon your life as you endeavor to walk in the fullness of God for your lives. I love you!

To my beautiful sister-in-laws:

Thank you for your encouraging words, I appreciate and love you for your care, concern, and support as I venture out in new things in God.

To my beautiful nieces & nephews:

Thank you! Auntie loves you! You can be ALL that God has called you to be. There is **no** limit to your potential in God. Go forth in God!

To my friends:

Thank you for all of your love and support. Continue to go forth in God in all things. I love you!

To my Pastors and Church family:

Thank you for your guidance, love, and support. I love and appreciate every word of encouragement that was sown in my life as I stepped out in ministry for more of what God called me into. I appreciate the uniqueness in each of you. I thank God for your many prayers. I love you!

To my Editing Committee and Web page designer:

I am so blessed to have such awesome people on my team. Thank you so much for seeing this project to completion. I thank God for your commitment and dedication. I love you and I am grateful for all that you have done. Together we accomplished much, thank you!

Most of all I would like to thank God for making all this possible, and for the many readers that shall read this book and grow thereof. I am grateful for life, health, and a strong mind; thank you God for empowering me to be whom you created me to be. I am grateful for each one of you as you allow the spirit of God to speak to your heart throughout this book. May you receive all that God has for you and your household in Jesus name. Amen.

Introduction

Are you ready to avail yourself unto the Lord; extending your loins, allowing the Spirit to use you, instruct you, and show you which direction to take? If so, *"13 . . . Gird up the loins of your mind, be sober, and rest your hope fully upon the grace that is to be brought to you at the revelation of Jesus Christ; 14 as obedient children, not conforming yourselves to the former lusts, as in your ignorance; 15 but as He who called you is holy, you also be holy in all your conduct" (1 Peter 1:13-15, NKJV)*. It's time to gird the loins of your mind, in other words, it's time to equip, to prepare yourself for action in all that Christ has for you. Are you ready to make the exchange? You can't continue to behave in accordance to your former ways. There is a higher call for you to be different in your actions and to be holy in your conduct. Will you journey with me throughout this book as we endeavor to keep building our life for Christ? As we build our life in Christ, He will make us into a beautiful vessel of honor, one that is prepared and equipped for every good work.

Christ is your overseer and He has the plans, process, and the ability to create in His hands, therefore, *2 Do not be conformed to this world, but be transformed by the renewing of your mind, that you may prove what is that good and acceptable and perfect will of God" (Romans 12:2, NKJV)*. As you attempt to build upon your foundation you are called not to be conformed to this world, but be transformed, be changed, by the renewing of your mind through the word of God. The word of God has the power to change your thinking and to destroy that old vessel with its destructive habits, therefore, making it imperative that you understand the word of God. Accepting and obeying the word of God brings revival, restoration, and the ability to resist the ploys, tactics, and schemes of the enemy.

The renewal of the mind should be a continual process throughout your life. It brings vigor and the ability to know the will of God, as you are being made into a beautiful vessel of honor.

- When life seems unfair and burdens begin to weigh you down, what do you do—Keep moving forward for your purpose awaits!
- When there are more problems than seem to be answers, what do you do—Keep moving forward!
- When your needs are met but desires are not, what do you do—Keep moving forward! Refuse to allow things to stop your purpose.

Can you continue to build and move forward no matter what life throws your way or do you take matters in your own hands and try to fix things? Often, people try different measures to ensure that things are smooth sailing in their lives but as a Christian you must learn to rely on the Lord trusting Him completely. Denying the flesh is never an easy or simple task. In the life of Leah and Rachel it was by no means an easy task to compete for the love and affection of their husband, Jacob. They were indeed the Lord's vessel but became marred in the hands of the potter.

^{16} Now Laban had two daughters: the name of the elder was Leah, and the name of the younger was Rachel. ^{17} Leah's eyes were delicate, but Rachel was beautiful of form and appearance. ^{18} Now Jacob loved Rachel; so he said, "I will serve you seven years for Rachel your younger daughter." ^{30} Then Jacob also went in to Rachel, and he also loved Rachel more than Leah . . . ^{31} When the LORD saw that Leah was unloved, He opened her womb; but Rachel was barren" (Genesis 29:16-18, 30-31, NKJV).

Jacob loved Rachel more than Leah. Leah desired for her husband to love her, whereas Rachel desired to give her husband a son. She had his love and attention but wanted more. Both ladies had desires and longings that were lingering within but did not know how to appease the desire, the vessels were marred. Often times because of the longings and urges someone experience within, they try to soothe and satisfy their needs in other ways, only to realize that the measure they took did not satisfy their urges and longings. So what should you do when desires are present but not met? Surely the Lord sees your condition, surely He does not want you to stay this way, and so what do you do? You begin trying to satisfy the flesh with extreme measures instead of taking it to the Lord in prayer. Communicate with the Lord concerning your desires; allow Him to work in your life creating you to be the vessel He has called you to be. Cast all your cares on Him for He cares for you. Remove yourself from the frustration and allow the Lord to work on your behalf. While He's working pray and mediate on His word allowing it to enrich you, making you into a beautiful vessel of honor.

The Lord opened Leah's womb, He saw that she was unloved and she began to have sons, hoping that somehow now her husband would love her. Giving him sons did not make him love her, but she received love from her sons. She conceived and bore the following to Jacob:

1st Son: And she said, "The Lord has surely seen my affliction, now he will love me."
2nd Son: "Because I am unloved, He gave me this son also."
3rd Son: "Now this time He will become attached to me because I have borne him three sons."
4th Son: She said, "Now I will praise the Lord, therefore she called him Judah which means praise," and then she stopped bearing.

Finally, Leah begins to build upon her foundation by praising the Lord. She realized she could not make her husband love her. Are you ready to speak to your situation as well? Are you tired of struggling with your situation only to see that it's not getting any better? Do you want more? If so, you must come to a place like Leah and realize this is it, now this time I will praise the Lord. In other words, this time I'm giving it all to the Lord. I don't have anything left in me to make him/her love me, to change my situation. I release myself totally and completely to God, therefore this time I'm going to praise the Lord. Is this your testimony on today? If you have done all you know to do and still things aren't getting any better, then sisters and brothers release it to the Lord. Refuse to live a defeated life any longer, a life that shows no sign of victorious living.

You are a mighty man/woman of valor and your labor in the Lord is not in vain. Your appointed time to be blessed is here, you are God's chosen vessel, and you shall reap if you do not faint or lose heart. The Lord has heard your prayers and a time of reaping shall spring forth. Hold firm to the truth of God's word and keep building your life in Christ. As you do, you shall rise to the level of potential that Christ is calling you to. A higher standard of living will cause your faith to increase. As you continue to build upon your foundation in the Lord, remember to "*⁵Trust in the Lord with all your heart, and lean not on your own understanding; ⁶in all your ways acknowledge Him and He shall direct your paths*" *(Proverbs 3:5-6, NKJV)*. You will be all that Christ has called you to be (a beautiful vessel).

SECTION I

DESTROYING THE THINGS OF OLD:

This section deals with the tearing down

process in an attempt to make a better vessel.

Chapter 1

A Lifestyle of a Twisted Mess

Sometimes in life things may get hectic and lead you into a state of confusion. However, if your foundation is built upon Christ you will be able to rise above any obstacle. Christ has empowered you with what you need to overcome all things. Do you walk around like everything is fine, as if you've got yourself together and there's no need for help from anyone? How often do you deal with the issues in your life? Well on today will you allow the Holy Spirit to minister to your heart and unlock the twisted mess and lies that hold you captive?

A lifestyle of a twisted mess consists of a defeated lifestyle, one that is twisted with lies and confusion. Satan is your opposing enemy and his desire is to destroy you and your family. He wants you to be twisted in your thinking, twisted in your actions, living beneath your birthright and missing out on your inheritance from the Lord. Satan is the father of lies; his goal is to offer you many things so that you can have a good time all the while leading you further and further away from the Lord. He will create ways, things, and people to make you enjoy sin, and have you to continue living a sinful lifestyle. At the expense of your soul, the devil will offer you suggestions with no rules, guidelines, or structure. He will twist the truth right before your eyes telling you its okay. You must remember *"20 For when you were slaves of sin, you were free in regard to righteousness. 21 But then what benefit (return) did you get from the things of which you are now ashamed? [None] for the end of those things is death"(Romans 6:20-21, AMP). "10The thief did not come except to steal, and to kill, and to destroy. I have come that they may have life, and that they may have it more abundantly" (John 10:10, NKJV).*

Satan's main objective is to keep you bound. He wants you to be a slave to sin, knowing very well that being a slave to sin leads to death. He does not want you to receive the freedom that Christ offers. There is so much you can attain while living your life for Christ. When I first started out in my life for Christ I was a twisted mess and the spirit began to reveal the truth to me. There is absolutely no way you can claim to know Christ and yet refuse to obey Him. As I share my testimony with you I pray it reveals something to you concerning your lifestyle and the message you are proclaiming. I pray that your speech matches your actions and your actions match your speech.

Oftentimes because you go to church for years, sit under a powerful teacher, attend Bible Study, Sunday school, and participate in various things in the church faithfully, you may begin to think you know Christ. You must understand, works do not qualify you as one who knows Him. You must take the time to establish a relationship with Jesus Christ, (get to know Him). Your works cannot and will not save you. The word says, *"21 Not everyone who says to me, 'Lord, Lord,' shall enter the kingdom of heaven, but he who does the will of My Father in heaven. 22 Many will say to Me in that day, 'Lord, Lord, have we not prophesied in Your name, cast out demons in Your name, and done many wonders in Your name?'* [23] *And then I will declare to them, 'I never knew you; depart from Me, you who practice lawlessness"* (Matthew 7:21-23, NKJV).

Even though you prophesied in His name, cast out demons in His name, performed many wonders in His name that does not qualify you as one that knows Him. He will say to you, *"Depart, go away because you have no self control, you are unruly and I don't even know you."* Do not allow these words to be spoken to you. You have time to get it right with the Lord. *John 10:3-5* States when you are known by Jesus and He is known to you, the following will be evident in your life. *"*[3] *To him the doorkeeper opens, and the sheep hear his voice; and He calls His own sheep by name and leads them out.* [4] *And when He brings out His own sheep, He goes before them; and the sheep follow Him, for they know His voice.* [5] *Yet they will by no means follow a stranger, but will flee from him, for they do not know the voice of strangers"* (NKJV). Whose voice are you following? Who is opening your door? If you are in the sheepfold you will follow the Shepherd and in following the Shepherd you will obey His word.

[1]**Know:** to know someone is to perceive directly, grasp in the mind with clarity or certainty. To regard as true beyond doubt. To have a practical understanding of, as through experience; be skilled in. To perceive as familiar; recognize, to be acquainted with, to be able to distinguish, to possess knowledge, understanding or information.

Do you have a practical understanding of who the Lord is? Are you acquainted with Him? Do you have a relationship with the Lord? It's time to be truthful about your relationship with the Lord. Do you spend time with the Lord reading your bible? When you read the bible do you perceive or understand what you've read? Do you allow what you've read to become a part of you; does it touch the core of your heart? What are your motives for reading? Is it for an outward show trying to appear knowledgeable? Search yourself and be honest because the Lord is well aware of how you spend your time. The Lord is aware of all the deeds and things you do. He wants you to be who He called you to be.

Even though you were created in iniquity,
you can still be who the Lord has called you to be.

Even though you were once a sinner (some are still sinners),
you can still be who the Lord has called you to be.

Even though you obey your flesh and your thoughts more than God's word,
you can still be who the Lord has called you to be.

Even though you don't know the Lord personally,
you can still be who the Lord has called you to be.

Even though you don't praise the Lord with all your heart,
you can still be who the Lord has called you to be.

Even though you don't worship the Lord in spirit and in truth,
you can still be who He has called you to be.

Even though you have not the mind of Christ,
you can still be who He has called you to be.

Even though you don't understand your life purpose,
you can still be who the Lord has called you to be.

It's time for you to be who the Lord says you are!

"*12 Therefore do not let sin reign in your mortal body so that you obey its evil desires. 13 Do not offer any part of yourself to sin as an instrument of wickedness, but rather offer yourselves to God as those who have been brought from death to life; and offer every part of yourself to him as an instrument of righteousness. 14 For sin shall no longer be your master, because you are not under the law, but under grace" (Romans 6:12-14, NIV).* You do not have to allow sin to rule you. You do not have to continue living a twisted lifestyle. You can change, you can be different, and it's all in the choices you make. Give yourself to the Lord so that you can do what is right. Sin will control you until you decide to stop giving in to it. Make up your mind that you will live a holy life and be set apart. "*19 I am using an example from everyday life because of your human limitations. Just as you used to offer yourselves as slaves to impurity and to ever-increasing wickedness, so now offer yourselves as slaves to righteousness leading to holiness" (Romans 6:19, NIV).* Being holy and set apart means you are living a life for Christ and not only in the presence of selective individuals, but at all times. His desire is not to see you as being a slave to unclean things and becoming more and more evil, but He wants you to be a slave to righteousness, right living, and doing what's right. In doing this you shall develop into that vessel of honor.

No matter what you choose to do in life or how you choose to do it, make sure you have a solid foundation in the Lord. Do not forsake His laws, bind them upon your heart and obey them. If you choose to live a wicked or twisted lifestyle please know there will be consequences behind your choices. In the life of Judah's son, and as a result of their wickedness and disobedience, their lives were taken from them. "*6 Judah took a wife for Er, his first-born and her name was Tamar. 7 But Er, Judah's first born was wicked in the sight of the Lord, and the Lord killed him. 8 And Judah said to Onan, 'Go in to your brother's wife and marry her, and raise up an heir to your brother. 9 But Onan knew that the heir would not be his; and it came to pass, when he went in to his brother's wife, that he emitted on the ground, lest he should give an heir to his brother. 10 And the thing which he did displeased the Lord; therefore he killed him also" (Genesis 38:6-10, NKJV).* We see here that because of Er's and Onan's behavior the Lord was displeased and as a result they were killed. You should always make sure your behavior is pleasing to the Lord. Walk in obedience to the word of the Lord; refuse to allow bitterness, unforgiveness, and evil thoughts to rest in your heart. Do not allow the pain of your past to hold you captive, never allowing you to accept the healing that Jesus so graciously offers.

Life is precious and you do not have time to continue living a twisted lifestyle. Release the hurt and bitterness so you can move on. As you develop your relationship with the Lord confess your sins daily, refuse to live in mess, and allow the Lord to change your mess into a miracle. Repent, turn from your sin, and make a conscious decision not to go back to it. Don't allow anyone or anything to keep you from doing what's right. *"³⁵ Who shall ever separate us from Christ's love? Shall suffering and affliction and tribulation? Or calamity and distress? Or persecution or hunger or destitution or peril or sword? ³⁶ Even as it is written, for thy sake we are put to death all the day long; we are regarded and counted as sheep for the slaughter ³⁷ Yet amid all these things we are more than conquerors and gain a surpassing victory through Him who loved us.³⁸ For I am persuaded beyond doubt (am sure) that neither death nor life, nor angels nor principalities, nor things impending and threatening nor things to come, nor powers,³⁹ Nor height nor depth, nor anything else in all creation will be able to separate us from the love of God which is in Christ Jesus our Lord"* (Romans 8:35-39, AMP). **Be determined not to allow sin, circumstances, lack or loss to separate you from Jesus' love.**

Are you one who is continuously rebellious and disobedient? Are you working in the sanctuary and yet refusing to acknowledge Him as Lord of your life? Are you faithful in attending Worship Service and Bible Study and yet refuse to adhere to what is being taught? Are you living a sinful life and think that it's ok because others are doing the same type of things? This behavior does not represent one who is created in the image of Christ. There is nothing about this behavior that causes Christ to smile upon your actions. Living the Christian life will cause a change to take place in you as you obey the word. Obeying the word will cause you to grow and become mature in the things of God. Your life will be a reflection of God's word. It's time to seek the Lord daily in all things.

In my life, when I attended Worship Service and Bible Study I found myself repenting of evil doings. The word found me in my mess and the Spirit dealt with me. Even though I was a mess the Lord did not give up on me. When I said I accepted Christ in my life, no one made me do it. I did not do it because I truly meant it, I did it because others did it and I did not want to be left out. So from that day until some time later in my life, I wore a mask saying, "yes, I'm saved." I refused to live by what I heard because I sure wasn't reading the bible. I was stinky and messy, and my sins that I committed were wrong. I willfully did things contrary to God's word. I may not have known his word to the full extent, but that which I knew, I refused to obey. I was living a messy lifestyle. I was not trying to change and I told myself that it was ok because others were doing the same things. It is never right to sin just because others are sinning.

The Lord continued to deal with me. I heard the word of God preached Sunday after Sunday and yet I refused to allow the word I heard to deliver me. He began to show me the filth that was living in me. My Pastor, Apostle Lewis began to call out my mess, the sin that I was entangled in, and explained how you do not have to live in sin. Sin is wrong and the Lord can deliver you. As I began to look at my life and the things that I was doing I had to come clean before the Lord. I had to get help; I had to rise up and out of the twisted lifestyle of sin that I had chosen.

As I continued to work in the church, and attended Bible Study faithfully something else came up. I had yet another problem. I knew my decision would be wrong but I made the decision anyway, I willingly chose to sin. One Sunday Apostle Lewis was getting ready to close the service and before he did he began to speak about my situation. He said, "Someone is about to make a decision and the Lord is against it, so you should not do it." But did I listen? No, because my mind was already made up and I felt it would be better for me this way. After that I was confronted with more issues. The Lord began to deal with me and I openly said, "Yes Lord I will do it again." Why? Because at that time in my life I was wearing a mask and sin did not phase me; it was my lifestyle! The outward duties showed salvation but my heart and actions were saying something different. As I continued on my misguided path I found myself doing things that were wrong over and over again without remorse.

The events in my life turned around when I truly repented and made my confession to the Lord. I began to diligently seek the Lord with all my heart. As you diligently seek the Lord, things will turn around for you as well. Begin to read your Bible and allow it to flush out the filth that holds you captive. As you examine your life and realize the areas that need changing, you need to do so immediately. As Christians one of our biggest mistakes is to recognize our sins, but refuse to deal with them. The events in our life happen for a reason. The Lord knows what is needed in order to draw water from each of his wells. The manner in which the Lord knows you is unfathomable, indescribable and almost seems unreal. Therefore you can not stop at this place; you must continue to build upon your foundation despite all obstacles.

As you look at your life what phase are you in your life? Are you committing sin willingly, or is your flesh and spirit warring against each other as Paul spoke about? *[14] We know that the law is spiritual; but I am unspiritual, sold as a slave to sin. [15] I do not understand what I do. For what I want to do I do not do, but what I hate I do. [16] And if I do what I do not want to do, I agree that the law is good. [17] As it is, it is no longer I myself who do it, but it is sin living in me. [18] For I know that good itself does not dwell in me, that is, in my sinful nature. For I have the desire to do what is good, but I cannot carry it out. [19] For I do not do the good I want to do, but the evil I do not want to do—this I keep on doing. [20] Now if I do what I do not want to do, it is no longer I who do it, but it is sin living in me that does it. [21] So I find this law at work: Although I want to do good, evil is right there with me. [22] For in my inner being I delight in God's law; [23] but I see another law at work in me, waging war against the law of my mind and making me a prisoner of the law of sin at work within me. [24] What a wretched man I am! Who will rescue me from this body that is subject to death"* (Romans 7:14-24, AMP)? We see that in the flesh nothing good dwells. You may have the desire to do good, but you do not do it. The evil that you do not want to do, this you keep doing. Why? Because *"[23] . . . I see another law at work in me, waging war against the law of my mind and making me a prisoner of the law of sin at work within me."* There is an inward war going on in your mind and it brings you into captivity to the sin that you allowed in your life. To combat sin you must repent, release it, and fill your mind with the word of God. Be consistent and persistent in spending time in the word. Commit to be a doer of the word and not a hearer only. Stop allowing your sin to bring you into captivity so much so that you are enslaved by it.

Now as you continue in taking an honest look at your life, what things are you persuaded to do even though it's wrong? How have you allowed your lifestyle to become a twisted mess? There is no good place the flesh can lead you to. *"¹⁸ For I know that nothing good dwells within me, that is, in my flesh. I can will what is right, but I cannot perform it. [I have the intention and urge to do what is right, but no power to carry it out]" (Romans 7:18, AMP).*

If you continue to choose to do wrong (sin), it leads to a separation between you and the Lord. It's time to stop the madness, make an effort to do better, to do right. *"⁵ Those who live according to the flesh have their minds set on what the flesh desires; but those who live in accordance with the Spirit have their minds set on what the Spirit desires. ⁶ The mind governed by the flesh is death, but the mind governed by the Spirit is life and peace. ⁷ The mind governed by the flesh is hostile to God; it does not submit to God's law, nor can it do so. ⁸ Those who are in the realm of the flesh cannot please God" (Romans 8:5-8, NIV).* Who are you pleasing?

Often times you try to build your life centered on what you think is best for you, excluding the Lord. You begin doing things in your strength only to see it crumble down without a base. You must allow the foundation to be laid first. Will you allow the Lord to complete the foundation in you as He destroys the things of old?

Many have been dealing with a filthy lifestyle for years whether it be lying, cheating, fornicating, backbiting, gossiping, filthy talking, stealing or adultery, it does not matter. What's important now is what will you do from this point on? Knowing that sin reigns in your life, what will you do? How will you continue to behave? You have been struggling with your twisted lifestyle long enough. You know your struggle but at this place in your life, as it applies to you it will act as a cleansing agent. Admit that you need help, offer true repentance for the place you have dwelt; a change will come. Jesus has promised to guide and instruct you in the way that you should go. Receive it now in Jesus' name. I pray you have released what has held you in captivity for years. And as you continue reading allow Jesus' healing virtue to remove your pain. In order to do better you have to do right. So in order to do right you must let it go!

Pray this prayer with me:
> Lord thank you for your grace and mercy. Forgive (insert your name) for his/her sin of (name your sin), I know it is wrong and I have been held in captivity by the spirit of (name your sin). Lord release its hold on my life now. I decree and declare I will be free from the spirit of (name your sin), I am free from all forms of bondage in Jesus name. Amen.

INSIGHT AND REVELATION

A Lifestyle of a Twisted Mess

The Lord can make a difference in your life as you release the mess to Him. Where will you allow this word to be sown in your life? Will you continue in mess or release it and let it go? *"³A sower went out to sow.⁴ And as he sowed, some seeds fell by the roadside, and the birds came and ate them up.⁵ Other seeds fell on rocky ground, where they had not much soil; and at once they sprang up, because they had no depth of soil.⁶ But when the sun rose, they were scorched, and because they had no root, they dried up and withered away.⁷ Other seeds fell among thorns, and the thorns grew up and choked them out.⁸ Other seeds fell on good soil, and yielded grain—some a hundred times as much as was sown, some sixty times as much, and some thirty"* (Matthew 13:3-8, AMP).

At this moment think about all the messages you've heard and all the books you've read. Where was it sown? Did it fall at the roadside, or on rocky ground? Did you allow it to take root in your heart, did it fall among thorns or did it fall on good soil and yield an increase?

You must understand Satan's purpose in your life. *"¹⁹ While anyone is hearing the Word of the kingdom and does not grasp and comprehend it, the evil one comes and snatches away what was sown in his heart. This is what was sown along the roadside.²⁰ As for what was sown on thin (rocky) soil, this is he who hears the Word and at once welcomes and accepts it with joy;²¹ Yet it has no real root in him, but is temporary (inconstant, lasts but a little while); and when affliction or trouble or persecution comes on account of the Word, at once he is caused to stumble [he is repelled and begins to distrust and desert Him Whom he ought to trust and obey] and he falls away.²² As for what was sown among thorns, this is he who hears the Word, but the cares of the world and the pleasure and delight and glamour and deceitfulness of riches choke and suffocate the Word, and it yields no fruit.²³ As for what was sown on good soil, this is he who hears the Word and grasps and comprehends it; he indeed bears fruit and yields in one case a hundred times as much as was sown, in another sixty times as much, and in another thirty"* (Matthew 13:19-23, AMP). Satan's desire is to destroy the word of God before it takes root in your life. He does not want the word sown in your heart.

As I take this moment to reflect over my life I can truly say that there were times when the word I heard fell by the wayside and the enemy snatched it away just as fast as I received it. Then there were times in my life when the word fell on stony places. I received the word with joy but only for a while and then when tribulation and persecution came I stumbled. As I look at my life now ten years later the word that I receive is sown on good ground. Now I can hear the word and understand the word and bear fruit. So as you look over your life complete the section below as to what the Lord has revealed to you about your relationship with Him.

Insight: The things that the spirit reveals to you at this point are very important to the making of a beautiful vessel. *"¹ Therefore, rid yourselves of all malice and all deceit, hypocrisy, envy, and slander of every kind. ² Like newborn babies, crave pure spiritual milk, so that by it you may grow up in your salvation"* (1 Peter 2: 1-2, NKJV).

TALK BACK:
Revelation: In your own words tell what the Lord revealed to you in this chapter.

Chapter 2

Mentality Check

"No more struggling"

To each of you God has given an unlimited amount of potential. He knows what you are capable of doing. But somewhere in life you decided to limit your potential, thinking, and abilities. In order to be all that God has created you to be, you must step outside of where you are right now. God formed you with a definite plan in mind and He is totally aware of whom He has called into existence in the earth realm. In order for you to understand who you were created to be, you need to examine the beginning. Prior to man's creation the following discussion was going on, *"²⁶ God said, let us [Father, Son, and Holy Spirit] make mankind in Our image, after Our likeness, and let them have complete authority . . ." (Genesis 1:26, AMP).* It was here that God began to put his plan in motion for mankind. He wanted mankind to be a reflection of himself walking in complete authority. He has given each of you unlimited potential. Despite where you are in life you were predestined for purpose. I speak to you now that you shall walk in the fullness of all that God has for you. You shall be all that He has created you to be. No more hindrances, whatever has happened, has happened, it's over, it's done, and it's time to move on and live the good life God has for you.

"⁵ Before I formed you in the womb I knew you" (Jeremiah 1:5, NKJV). The Lord knew you before you were conceived and formed in your mother's womb. He had knowledge of you and knew what you were capable of producing. He knows what you have already produced and what you will produce in the future. He knows you; your life has been predestined.

God has the plan; he sees your future, so seek Him. *"¹¹ For I know the thoughts that I think towards you says the Lord, thoughts of peace and not of evil, to give you a future and a hope" (Jeremiah 29:11, NKJV).* Your future is looking brighter everyday according to God's word. No longer will you struggle or wrestle with ideas, things, or people who have no confidence in you. It's time to stop fighting and struggling with the plans God has for your life. God has equipped you with what you need to live and produce what He has created you to produce.

It's time to move forward and in order to do so you need to understand your struggle within. Are you fearful, do you lack confidence, have you been rejected or denied? Do you struggle with a poor mentality? If so, anyone of these can cause you to struggle within, therefore finding it hard to believe the promises of God for your life. Stop allowing the tactics of the enemy to keep you from walking in the blessings God has for you. He knew you prior to conception and knew what you were called to do within your life time. Therefore, stop allowing who you think you are to hinder the move of God from operating in your life. I bind up fear and rejection in the name of Jesus. I bind up the poor mentality, thinking of yourself as less than who you really are. I bind up your lack of confidence, the unhealthy view of yourself. I apply the blood of Jesus over all areas that has hindered your process for the kingdom. I speak to you now, ARISE and SHINE for this is a new day, this is a new season, and this is your day to be better in the name of Jesus. Sons and daughters of the King, arise in your thinking, arise in your living, and arise in your speaking, for this is a NEW day in your life.

Spirit of fear I command you to release them now in the name of Jesus. The Spirit of fear shall not hinder the life that God has ordained for you. You have been given the ability to achieve, spirit of fear leave in the name of Jesus, you will no longer control my mind, my actions or my speech. "*[7] For God has not given us a spirit of fear, but of power, of love and a sound mind*" (*2 Timothy 1:7, NKJV*).

Spirit of rejection I command you to leave now in the name of Jesus. I take authority over the spirit of rejection, it will no longer control or direct my life. You shall be all that God has called you to be in the name of Jesus. "*[27] Leave no [such] room or foothold for the devil [give no opportunity to him]*" (*Ephesians 4:27, AMP*).

Spirit of Negative thinking I command you to leave now in the name of Jesus. On today choose to take every thought captive and "*[5] Let this mind be in you which was also in Christ Jesus*" (*Philippians 2:5, NKJV*). Refuse to allow the devil to feed you lies and to manipulate your life, you are worth more than that. Lord release your sons and daughters from their negative mindset in the name of Jesus. "*[23] Be renewed in the spirit of your mind*" (*Ephesians 4:23, NKJV*).

Spirit of lacking confidence I command you to leave now in the name of Jesus. You must have confidence in your abilities so that you can create and be all thatGod has called you to be. "*[37] . . . we are more than conquerors and gain a surpassing victory through Him who loved us*" (*Romans 8:37, AMP*). "*[6] . . . being confident of this very thing, that He who begun a good work in you will complete it until the day ofChrist Jesus . . .*" (*Philippians 1:6, NKJV*).

Stop struggling and fighting with that which is unseen, and unclear, get up and move forward. No longer will you live a life that views only the outer appearance. Let us examine the inner realm. Lord help us to see what you see both seen and unseen. No longer will you allow your potential to lie dormant, struggling and wrestling for lack of true understanding. Arise; this is your new day!

MY PRAYER OF FORGIVENESS

At this moment forgive thy servant for thinking of thyself as less than what you've said.
Forgive thy servant for wrestling and struggling with your plans for my life.
Forgive thy servant for straying out of thy will and running in the opposite direction.
Forgive thy servant for neglecting thy people and refusing to obey.
Forgive thy servant for following thy own agenda and for thinking selfishly.
Lord forgive thy servant in your unique and special way, that only you can.

You will no longer be fearful of the unknown. From this day forward you shall rejoice in the unknown, rejoice because you know that you are in the hands of the Almighty King. He's able to keep you in perfect peace so rest in Him. During moments when things become chaotic and you can't seem to find any answers know that God is in control. He is aware of your situation. "*4 Behold, He who keeps Israel, shall neither slumber nor sleep*" *(Psalm 121:4, NKJV). "6 Alleluia! For the Lord God Omnipotent reigns" (Revelation 19:6, NKJV)!* He has the ability and power to do whatever He wills. "*26 . . . With men this is impossible; but with God all things are possible*" *(Matthew 19:26, NKJV). "27 Behold, I am the Lord, the God of all flesh. Is there any thing too hard for Me" (Jeremiah 32:27, NKJV)? "37 For with God nothing will be impossible" (Luke 1:37, NKJV).* Whatever God has placed before you, He has also given you the ability to complete. No one will be able to stop what God is calling you forth to do. Go forth for you are sons and daughters of the King.

I am reminded about the calling of Gideon, and how he struggled to do what was asked of him. He was indeed a reflection of God's creation yet struggled with the call on his life. Gideon was created in God's image and likeness. He was a man who did not know the potential that was lying on the inside of him. Gideon was chosen to help the children of Israel during their cry for help. The Lord saw fit to use Gideon for such an occasion and He began to awaken that dead man mentality that had become a part of him. The Lord had great plans for Gideon's life. I don't know where you are in life but I call your spirit man to wake up, get up from the dead stuff, you are a vessel of honor and God has more for you. There is greatness on the inside of you.

> *11 Now the Angel of the LORD came and sat under the terebinth tree which was in Ophrah, which belonged to Joash the Abiezrite, while his son Gideon threshed wheat in the winepress, in order to hide it from the Midianites. 12 And the Angel of the LORD appeared to him, and said to him, "The LORD is with you, you mighty man of valor!" 13 Gideon said to Him, "O my lord, if the LORD is with us, why then has all this happened to us? And where are all His miracles which our fathers told us about, saying, 'Did not the LORD bring us up from Egypt?' But now the LORD has forsaken us and delivered us into the hands of the Midianites."14 Then the LORD turned to him and said, "Go in this might of yours, and you shall save Israel from the hand of the Midianites. Have I not sent you?"15 So he said to Him, "O my Lord,[b] how can I save Israel? Indeed my clan is the weakest in Manasseh, and I am the least in my father's house."16 And the LORD said to him, "Surely I will be with you, and you shall defeat the Midianites as one man" (Judges 6:11-16, NKJV).*

The Lord had more for Gideon's life. He spoke to the mighty man in Gideon, but he failed to see himself as a mighty man of valor; he did not see what the angel of the Lord saw. The Lord saw Gideon's triumph over the enemy's camp when He told him to go. He said, "Your provider, Eli Shaddai, Eli Rohi, and the Great Jehovah is in company with you, for you are a powerful, great, and strong man with courage, guts, and the boldness needed to free my people." Gideon responded, "Who, me, how can I save them? I am the weakest and the least in my father's house so how do you expect to use me for such a great task?" Gideon questioned the instructions and began to tell the Lord his view of himself as if the Lord did not already know the vessel that He had formed. *13 Gideon said to Him,*

*"O my lord, if the L*ORD *is with us, why then has all this happened to us? And where are all His miracles which our fathers told us about, saying, 'Did not the L*ORD *bring us up from Egypt?' But now the L*ORD *has forsaken us and delivered us into the hands of the Midianites."* You see the children of Israel were in a difficult situation at the time when the Lord appeared to Gideon. He was actually hiding wheat for future purposes from the enemy. This is the son of the King who owns everything; yet found himself in a low place for a season. Even though Gideon was in a low place, it was not over, it was not his end. God had a greater plan and it included what He placed on the inside of Gideon. You need to shake yourself and know that God has a greater plan for you and it includes what He has placed on the inside of you. Sons and daughters of the King you have the ability to accomplish great things so stop seeing yourself as the weakest link. You can do all things with God's help. You will no longer see yourself as the weaker vessel or the least. You will see yourself through the eyes of Christ.

"¹ Fear not, for I have redeemed you; I have called you by your name; you are mine" (Isaiah 43:1, NKJV).

*"² This is what the L*ORD *says He who made you, who formed you in the womb, and who will help you: Do not be afraid, Jacob, my servant, . . . whom I have chosen" (Isaiah 44:2, NIV).*

"² You are a holy people to the Lord your God, and the Lord has chosen you to be a people for Himself, a special treasure above all the peoples who are on the face of the earth" (Deuteronomy 14:2, NKJV).

"²⁰ We are ambassadors of Christ" (2 Corinthians 5:20, NKJV).

"¹² Yet to all who received Him, to those who believed in His name, He gave the right to become children of God" (John 1:12, NIV).

"¹⁶ You did not choose Me, but I chose you and appointed you that you should go and bear fruit, and that your fruit should remain, that whatever

You ask of the Father in my name He may give you" (John 15:16, NKJV).

"¹⁰ For we are God's handiwork, created in Christ Jesus to do good works, which God prepared in advance for us to do" (Ephesians 2:10, NIV).

"¹² In Him and through faith in Him we may approach God with freedom and confidence" (Ephesians 3:12, NIV).

Stop allowing the enemy to give you defeated thoughts about yourself. Who you are now is not all of who you will be. You need to see yourself as who God has created you to be.

INSIGHT AND REVELATION

Mentality Check *"No more struggling"*

As sons and daughters of the King, arise and be who you were created to be. Stop struggling in your thinking. *"² Do not conform to the pattern of this world, but be transformed by the renewing of your mind. Then you will be able to test and approve what God's will is—His good, pleasing and perfect will"* (Romans 12:2, NIV).

God will transform you into a new person by changing the way you think. Renewing your mind with the word of God will change the essence of your being. Then you will learn God's will for your life, because you will be walking in alignment with His word.

I have not always seen myself as a daughter of the King. It took me years to get to that place to know who I was in Christ. The enemy was forever present trying to deceive, and disturb my life. He tries to weave me into his web of lies, schemes, and deception at any opportunity he can. While looking over my life I realize things happened for a greater purpose of which I was not aware. The events in my life were to make me a better vessel, one that was fit for the King. *"¹³ You made all the delicate, inner parts of my body and knit me together in my mother's womb.¹⁴ Thank you for making me so wonderfully complex! Your workmanship is marvelous—how well I know it"* (Psalm 139:13-14, NLT).

Insight: The things that the spirit reveals to you at this point are very important to the making of a beautiful vessel. *"⁹ You are a chosen generation, a royal priesthood, a holy nation, His own special people"* (1 Peter 2:9, NKJV).

TALK BACK:
Revelation: In your own words tell what the Lord revealed to you in this chapter.

_____

_____

_____

_____

_____

_____

_____

_____

_____

_____

_____

_____

_____

_____

_____

_____

Chapter 3

Don't Waste Your Goods

"The Importance of the Right Connections"

God has a plan and a purpose for your life. No matter what the enemy has told you God wants you to know, "There is a plan for you." So I encourage you on today, don't waste your goods. *"¹⁰ The thief does not come except to steal, and to kill, and to destroy. I have come that they may have life, and that they may have it more abundantly (to the full, overflowing)" (John 10:10, NKJV).* The devil shows up in your life to do one of three things at a moments notice, which is to steal, to kill and to destroy you. He not only desires for you to waste your goods, but he connects you with the wrong people. Then he uses them against you to kill your dreams and vision, to steal your joy and peace, and to destroy your hope. But sons and daughters of the King God has a different plan. He wants you to enjoy everything in your life, your relationships (marriage), your family and friends, your job (career), your teachers (instructors) and your ministry. The devil seeks opportunity to destroy the things that God wants you to enjoy. I encourage you my sisters and brothers, don't waste your goods playing with the devil. God has something better for you. He has promised you a life of abundance. Are you willing to release the wrong connections in order to become that vessel of honor?

The gifts, talents, and abilities on the inside of you are there for a purpose. **You were created with the ability to produce great things.** *"²⁷ So God created man in His own image; in the image of God He created him; male and female He created them" (Genesis 1:27, NKJV).*

You have been created in God's image; His seeds of greatness are inside of you. Because God's seeds are on the inside of you, you can produce what He called you to produce. I encourage you on today not to waste, or throw away your goods like the prodigal son. *In Luke 15:13, NKJV . . . "The younger son gathered all together, journeyed to a far country, and there wasted his possessions with prodigal living."* This son's actions reflected that he did what he thought was right in his sight. He gathered all he had and left home in search of something better. Only to find within time he had wasted his possessions living a lifestyle that was not meant to be. But yet he found his way back home, and was able to recover and get the right connections. If you are reading this book you too can find your way back home and get the right connections. Your life is not over no matter what you have wasted or loss. God's plan for you can still come to pass. You will become that beautiful vessel of honor.

I am reminded of the life of King Solomon and how he allowed his heart to be connected to the wrong things. God had great plans for his life but he allowed his heart to connect with that which was forbidden. Have you allowed your heart to be connected to those forbidden things? Do the people you connect with cause your creativity, dreams, vision, gifts and abilities to grow, flourish, and to leap within you? Or do they bring about death and inactivity in your life, producing nothing? Check your connections. You need to be connected to people that will add life to your dreams, visions, talents, skills and abilities. How long will you continue to waste your goods on dead things that come to steal, kill, and destroy you? You have to make a decision. I pray that by the time you get to the end of this chapter the Holy Spirit will reveal to you the things you need to release from your life.

I speak to the king in you to take your rightful place, I command you to go forth and be all that God created you to be. Lord cleanse their minds with your word bringing about a change in their mindset which affects their actions and their lifestyle. Help them to see the importance of the right connections in their life. I decree and declare that the eyes of their spirit function with 20/20 vision for understanding, knowledge, and clarity concerning the people involved in their life and that their ears would be in tune to your spirit. Now *"17 Lord open their eyes so they can see (2 Kings 6:17) you in all things*," in Jesus name. Amen.

King Solomon had great riches, *"23 He was greater in riches and wisdom than all the other kings of the earth. 24 The whole world sought audience with Solomon to hear the wisdom God had put in his heart. Year after year everyone who came brought gifts articles of silver and gold, robes, weapons and spices, and horses and mules" (1 Kings 10:23-25, NIV)*. People sought to hear the wisdom that "GOD" put in Solomon's heart. The whole world wanted to hear from King Solomon. There was greatness on the inside of Solomon and because of this greatness people blessed him with gifts. We see that it was "GOD" who put the wisdom in his heart . . . God had a plan.

Even though he had riches and wisdom he had to obey God's instructions. It was God who had the plan. *"4 As for you, if you walk before me faithfully with integrity of heart and uprightness as David your father did, and do all I command and observe my decrees and laws, 5 I will establish your royal throne over Israel forever. 6 . . . But if you or your descendants turn away from me and do not observe the commands and decrees I have given you and go off to serve other gods and worship them, 7 then I will cut off Israel from the land . . ." (1 Kings 9:4-7, NIV)*.

King Solomon had a choice, either he could obey and all would be well forever, or he could refuse, turn away from the Lord and be cut off. You must realize the importance of obeying the word of God in your life. Obedience brings blessings upon your life; disobedience brings death. Sons and daughters of the King despite your riches and wisdom be mindful of your connections. Don't waste your goods! Do not allow it to cause you to be cut off from the King forever.

"1 King Solomon, however, loved many foreign women. 2 . . . They were from nations about which the Lord had told the Israelites, "You must not intermarry with them, because they will surely turn your hearts after their gods." Nevertheless, Solomon held fast to them in love. 3 He had seven hundred wives of royal birth and three hundred concubines, and his wives led him astray. 4 As Solomon grew old, his

wives turned his heart after other gods, and his heart was not fully devoted to the Lord his God, as the heart of David his father had been" (1 Kings 11: 1-4, NIV).

King Solomon desired those whom the Lord told him not to marry. He held fast to them in love, he was connected to what was forbidden. He allowed himself to be connected to the enemy, connected to things that killed his love for God. Have you connected yourself with people that are forbidden, those whom you should not be in a relationship with? Have you allowed your heart to connect with someone that kills your love for God? Who or what have you allowed to kill your dream, your vision? Are you involved with someone else's mate? Have you given your heart to someone that the Lord has told you to cut off? Don't allow your affection for what is forbidden to turn your heart away from God. Check your connections, don't waste your goods, you are better than that.

King Solomon's wives led him astray as he grew old. They turned his heart after other gods. He allowed the enemy to come in and steal his heart from the one and only true God. He was connected to what was forbidden and as a result, *"9 The Lord became angry with Solomon because his heart had turned away from the Lord, the God of Israel, who had appeared to him twice. 10 Although he had forbidden Solomon to follow other gods, Solomon DID NOT keep the Lord's command" (1 King 11:9-10, NIV).* Sons and daughters of the King don't waste your goods; don't allow that which is forbidden, to turn your heart away from the Lord. Check your connections. If your connections are killing your vision and your love for Christ then release them, cut them off. The devil's desire *is to steal, kill and destroy (John 10:10, NKJV).* He will do all he can to control you to make you do the opposite of God's word. Don't allow him to knock you off the path that God has destined for your life.

"11 As a result of Solomon's decision "The Lord said to Solomon, since this is your attitude and you HAVE NOT kept my covenant and my decrees, which I commanded you, I will most certainly tear the kingdom away from you and give it to one of your subordinates" (1 Kings 11:11, NIV).

There was a result to Solomon's decision. Because of his disobedience the kingdom would be taken away from him. Every act of disobedience brings a result in your life. Don't waste your goods, check your connections now! If your connections have been forbidden by God then you must release them now. Ask yourself, what's in this for me to hang onto dead things? Think about it, what is in it for you?

You know you are connected to dead stuff but yet you refuse to let it go and cut it off. You must make a decision to release it **all** to the Lord. If it is forbidden release it now! Every connection that seeks to kill your dreams and vision release it now in the name of Jesus. Every connection that brings death that seeks to steal your heart away from God release it now in the name of Jesus. No longer will you compromise your life to have your way; instead seek to grow closer to the Lord. And as you do, He can help you to reject those things that are not good for you. You will no longer live a limited life because of your sins. Limited thinking brings low life. *"7Let the wicked forsake his way, and the* *unrighteous man his thoughts; let him return to the Lord, and He will have mercy on him . . ." (Isaiah 55:7, NJKV).*

Don't waste your goods, check your connections. *"³³ Do not be deceived; evil company corrupts good habits. ³⁴ Awake to righteousness and do not sin . . ." (1 Corinthians 15:33-34, NKJV).* Wake up! Open your eyes and see who is among you. Sons and daughters of the King do not be deceived. Stop accepting what is false by misrepresentation. Evil company (connections) corrupts (ruins) good habits. Don't allow your companions to ruin your good habits. Look at what you are doing! This call is for you to awake to righteousness and do not sin. This is not the lifestyle for you. You are worth much more.

If you want to do better you have to do right. The problem comes in when you decide within yourself that you do not want to do what is right. Then you get mad and upset when you find yourself in a mess. You have then allowed sin to crouch at your door. *"⁷If you do what is right, will you not be accepted? But if you do not do what is right, sin is crouching at your door; it desires to have you, but you must rule over it" (Genesis 4:7, NIV).* Some are in a terrible state because they failed to do what was right; therefore they allowed sin to crouch at their door. It requires an attitude of doing what is right in the sight of God and as you do, you will be accepted. If sin is harbored in your life, it dwells in your house; it waits at your door waiting to attach itself to you and your family as a means to destroy you. Make the decision now to release it and let it go. If it's not good for you, let it go, don't waste your goods; God has something better for you.

He said, *"¹ Blessed is the one who does not walk in step with the wicked or stand in the way that sinners take or sit in the company of mockers, ² but whose delight is in the law of the Lᴏʀᴅ, and who meditates on his law day and night. ³ That person is like a tree planted by streams of water, which yields its fruit in season and whose leaf does not wither whatever they do prospers" (Psalm 1: 1-3, NKJV).*

Check your connections, are you walking in the counsel of the wicked, living and doing the things that they do? This gives the enemy an open door in your life to influence you in many ways. Are you standing in the way of sinners, so closely related to them that you are participating in their sinful behaviors? Are you saying one thing with your mouth but doing something completely different with your body? Where are you standing? Are you sitting in the seat of mockers, hanging out with those who mock the things of God? If so then you need to know there is help and healing for you. Do you delight and meditate in the word of God? Delighting in the word of God brings satisfaction and yields spiritual growth. Meditating on the word is constantly thinking about the word and allowing it to shape your thoughts and actions. As you soak in God's presence daily it helps you to establish the right connections causing your dreams and vision to live.

When you do these things you shall be like a tree that is firmly planted by streams of water. Obeying the word of God causes you to be firmly planted in position for Christ, while yielding fruit in season and whose leaf does not wither despite the circumstances in your life. You shall be productive and yield an increase. Whatever you do, it shall prosper, thrive, and flourish. Why? Because you made the decision to stop wasting your goods and become connected to the right people.

Prayer:

> Lord, we come to you now in the name of Jesus asking you to cleanse our ways. As we obey your word, cover our minds with your blood and cleanse all darkness and all thoughts that are contrary to your will for our life. We ask you Lord to shut any doors that need to be shut and to open any doors that need to be opened. Give us knowledge, clarity, and understanding in all that we do in Jesus name. Amen.

INSIGHT AND REVELATION

Don't Waste Your Goods *"The Importance of the Right Connections"*

Make the decision that you will not continue to waste your goods. From this point forward release it all to the Lord.

Shh, Shh Allow God

Only God can fix what is broken and within time He will mend your heart.
Shh, Shh, sit down, be still, be quiet and let the healing begin.

God allowed this situation to arise now allow Him to mend your heart.
Allow Him to ease your pain.
Allow Him to show you the next step.
Please my child allow God!

Shh, Shh, sit down, be still, be quiet and allow God!

Never focus on what could have been, what one should have done, instead allow God.
Will you sit down and get quiet before Him this day?
Will you allow Him to mend, correct, rebuke, and revenge?
Will you allow God?

How can you mend what God has allowed to be broken?
Do you see why you were broken? Why?

Sit down, be still, be quiet, and focus only on your life and what's going on with you.
Ask God for He has your answer, He has what you need.
So my question was will you allow God?

Insight: The things that the spirit reveals to you at this point are very important to the making of a beautiful vessel. *"⁹ How can a young man cleanse his way? By taking heed according to your word" (Psalm 119:9, NKJV).*

TALK BACK:
Revelation: In your own words tell what the Lord revealed to you in this chapter.

_____
_____
_____
_____
_____
_____
_____
_____
_____
_____
_____
_____
_____
_____
_____
_____
_____
_____
_____
_____
_____
_____
_____
_____
_____
_____
_____
_____
_____
_____
_____
_____
_____
_____
_____
_____

SECTION II

KEYS FOR FOUNDATION BUILDING:

This section deals with laying the foundation for your life in Christ.

Chapter 4

Answering the Call

"Walking in the light"

Will you accept God's calling on your life? Will you accept God's free gift of eternal life? Will you say yes no matter what? How will you answer the call? *"⁶ Jesus answered, "I am the way and the truth and the life. No one comes to the Father except through me"* (John 14:6 NIV).

God said, "I've been calling you since you were formed. I have ordained you to come into existence. I have established you for my purpose. When will you see me, when will you obey me?

What will you do when you receive the call? What will happen when you receive the call? What will you do?

The caller may ask or tell you a number of things, but what will you be doing? What will you be doing before you receive the call? What will you say to the caller?

Will you be partying, gambling, cheating, or stealing? Will you be praying, fasting, or praising God? What will you be doing?

God said, "You will not know the day nor the hour for He's coming like a thief in the night." Will you be ready before God makes His final call for your life?

Admit You Have Sinned: *"²³For all have sinned, and fall short of the glory of God"* (Romans 3:23, NKJV).

Believe In The Lord Jesus: *"¹⁶ For God so loved the world that He gave His only begotten Son, that whosoever **believes in Him should not perish**, but have everlasting life"* (John 3:16, NKJV).

Confess with your Mouth: *"⁹ . . . if you confess with your mouth, **the Lord Jesus**,' and believe in your heart that **God raised Him from the dead**, you will **be saved.** ¹⁰For with the heart one believes unto righteousness and with the mouth confession is made unto salvation. ¹³Whoever calls on the name of the Lord shall be saved"* (Romans 10:9, 10, 13, NKJV). It is with the heart that man believes with the mouth that confession is made unto salvation. As you believe and make your confession, it shall become a reality in your life.

Say this prayer believing with all your heart:
> Lord, I understand I am a sinner, and I need a Savior. I believe that you died on the cross and rose on the third day to pay my sin debt. Please come into my life and

forgive my sins, and make me a new person. From this day forward I will put all my trust in you. Lord show me how to live a Christian life In Jesus Name. Amen.

I rejoice with your decision! Do not allow anyone to count you out for God has accepted you. What God has accepted, no man can alter. Welcome to the Kingdom!

Now as you walk in your new life with Christ it is imperative that you grow in the things of God. Your growth level depends upon your ability to comprehend and obey the Scriptures. Your faith will grow as your understanding of Gods' word grows. *"¹⁷Faith comes by hearing and hearing by the Word of God" (Romans 10:17, NKJV).* For the word of God is the incorruptible seed, that will always produce and never fail.

"²⁸ . . . Blessed are those who hear the word of God and keep it" (Luke 11:28, NKJV)! When you keep His word it means you are retaining and storing it. It allows you to be free in ministry to flow in the things of God. It empowers you to prosper. In the natural sense when you keep or store something you know what it is that you are keeping. So in the spiritual sense, when you keep or store the testimonies of God, you allow the word of God to be stored in your heart.

"¹¹ Your Word I have hidden in my heart that I might not sin against you" (Psalm 119:11, NKJV). Hiding the word in your heart is not about keeping it a secret from others, but it helps to keep you from sinning and gives you hope. It's hidden where no one can take it away. It's like storing treasure in your heart where the world is benefited and where Christ is being formed in you to bring about a change in your life. The word also helps to turn hateful and spiteful people into loving, peaceful, and easy going Christians. When you have been treated unfairly and you are unable to read the Bible, your heart will furnish you with what you need. The word you have hidden in your heart will be readily available at all times. In order to hide the word in your heart you must HEAR IT, RECEIVE IT, MEDITATE ON IT, and MEMORIZE IT!

"² Blessed are those who keep His testimonies, seek Him with the whole heart" (Psalm 119:2, NKJV). When you seek something it means to search for or to inquire of. When you search for and inquire of the Lord with your whole heart you are putting your heart, soul, and mind into what you are doing. This brings the blessing of God in your life. Look at what happens when you seek the Lord with your whole heart.

"¹² Then they entered into a covenant to seek the Lord God of their fathers with all their heart and with all their soul. ¹⁵ And all Judah rejoiced at the oath, for they had sworn with all their heart and sought Him with all their soul; and He was found by them, and the Lord gave them rest all around" (2 Chronicles 15:12, 15; NKJV).

We see here that Judah made a covenant to seek the Lord with all their heart and soul. As a result, the Lord was found by them, and the Lord gave them rest all around. He gave them what they needed. In 1 Samuel chapter 1 it talks about how Hannah earnestly and persistently sought the Lord for a son. She poured out her soul before the Lord and He remembered her and gave her a son. Her seeking was not in vain. When you seek something or someone it requires you to spend time with them. You have to put your time in, for the scripture states, *"He is a rewarder of those who diligently seek Him" (Hebrews 11:6, NKJV).* When you diligently seek the Lord you are making a consistent and constant effort to seek Him, and as you do you will be rewarded.

In Isaiah chapter 38 Hezekiah was also found seeking the Lord. Hezekiah became ill and was at the point of death. He received the message, "Get your house in order for you are going to die, you shall not recover." Hezekiah did not whine or complain about what the Lord said; instead he immediately began to seek the Lord through prayer. And the Lord heard his prayer and sent him another message, "I will add fifteen years to your life." Because Hezekiah sought the Lord the Lord gave him what he desired.

In your life are you diligent in seeking the Lord? Has He given you the desires of your heart? As you seek the Lord with all your heart and soul He will be found by you. Are you in need of a healing then the Lord is able to heal you. It does not matter how long you have been sick, the promise is, *"By His stripes you are healed" (Isaiah 53:5, NKJV).* Even though Hezekiah was at the point of death and was told he would not recover, look at the Lord's response. He gave him an additional fifteen years to his life. I speak to those who are in need of a healing on today. The Lord is able to heal you. *"His word will not return unto Him void" (Isaiah 55:11, NKJV).* Stand on the promises of God for your healing. *"He sent His word and healed them, and delivered them from their destruction" (Psalm 107:20, KJV).* He said, *"I am the Lord who heals you" (Exodus 15:26, NKJV).* Walk in your healing.

Do you need to be restored? He is able to restore everything that you lost; your life is not over. He can give you double for your trouble. *"This day I'm declaring a double bonus—everything you lost returned twice-over" (Zechariah 9:12, MSG)!* Regardless of how difficult things may be in your life, God can transform your mess into a message. What looks like demotion can be a promotion. Everything that you lost you can receive back double. Walk in your promise.

Are you in need of guidance or direction? Does your life seem a bit chaotic and confused? Then seek the Lord for He has all power and can enlighten you concerning the affairs of your life. *The Lord says, "I will guide you along the best pathway for your life. I will advise you and watch over you" (Psalm 32:8, NLT)!* All you have to do is follow the Lord's leading. He is the great overseer, whose eyes overlook everything. He knows the best pathway for your life and has promised to watch over you. *Job 36:7 "He does not take his eyes off the righteous; He enthrones them with kings and exalts them forever" (NIV).* He constantly observes the righteous no matter where they are, by supplying them with what they need. They are enthroned with Kings and He exalts them forever. Receive your blessing! Whatever you are in need of seek the Lord for He will manifest His heart to you as you learn to seek Him with all your heart and soul.

"². . . The Lord is with you while you are with Him. If you seek Him, He will be found by you; but if you forsake Him, He will forsake you" (2 Chronicles 15:2, NKJV). In this verse, it does not say He may be found by you, but He will be found by you if you seek

Him. It also lets you know if you forsake Him, then He has no choice but to forsake you. When you make the decision to leave the Lord outside of your circumstances and dilemma, you will make a mess. Look what happened when Judas left the Lord outside of his decision compared to the three Hebrew boys who left the Lord in their decision. Judas got caught up in a mess; he killed himself, died without the Lord. The three Hebrew boys were in a mess but the Lord was in the midst of the fire with them and no harm was done to them. So REMEMBER: ***The Lord is with you while you are with Him. If you seek Him, He will be found by you; but if you forsake Him, He will forsake you!"*** You have a choice will you continue to walk in the light growing in Christ?

A mature Christian realizes that the more they grow in the things of God and walk in the light there may be a special anointing on their life. God begins to reveal His plan for their life, ***"¹¹ For I know the plans I have for you," declares the LORD, "plans to prosper you and not to harm you, plans to give you hope and a future" (Jeremiah29:11, NIV.*** Unusual (strange) circumstances surrounded the anointing of David as king. It was during a time when their present king was still alive but rejected. The Lord commissioned Samuel to go to Jesse's house and anoint the next king. It was David's time to do more, God was seeking David's anointing for a greater task. For David was a vessel of honor sanctified and useful for the Master, prepared for every good work.

> *"¹ Now the LORD said to Samuel, "How long will you mourn for Saul, seeing I have rejected him from reigning over Israel? Fill your horn with oil, and go; I am sending you to Jesse the Bethlehemite. For I have provided Myself a king among his sons." ⁴ So Samuel did what the LORD said, and went to Bethlehem. And the elders of the town trembled at his coming, and said, "Do you come peaceably?" ⁵ And he said, "Peaceably; I have come to sacrifice to the LORD. Sanctify yourselves, and come with me to the sacrifice." Then he consecrated Jesse and his sons, and invited them to the sacrifice. ⁶ So it was, when they came, that he looked at Eliab and said, "Surely the LORD's anointed is before Him!" ⁷ But the LORD said to Samuel, "Do not look at his appearance or at his physical stature, because I have refused him. For the LORD does not see as man sees; for man looks at the outward appearance, but the LORD looks at the heart." ⁸ So Jesse called Abinadab, and made him pass before Samuel. And he said, "Neither has the LORD chosen this one." ⁹ Then Jesse made Shammah pass by. And he said, "Neither has the LORD chosen this one." ¹⁰ Thus Jesse made seven of his sons pass before Samuel. And Samuel said to Jesse, "The LORD has not chosen these." ¹¹ And Samuel said to Jesse, "Are all the young men here?" Then he said, "There remains yet the youngest, and there he is, keeping the sheep." And Samuel said to Jesse, "Send and bring him. For we will not sit down till he comes here." ¹² So he sent and brought him in. Now he was ruddy, with bright eyes, and good-looking. And the LORD said, "Arise, anoint him; for this is the one!" ¹³ Then Samuel took the horn of oil and anointed him in the midst of his brothers; and the Spirit of the LORD came upon David from that day forward. So Samuel arose and went to Ramah" (1 Samuel 16:1, 4-13, NKJV).*

As Samuel went to do what the Lord commanded, he looked at Eliab, one of Jesse's sons' and said surely the Lord's anointed is before him; surely he is the one. Why?

28

Samuel felt he was the one due to his outward appearances, his physical stature. The Lord immediately told Samuel, *"Do not look at his appearance or at his physical stature, because I have refused him. For the LORD does not see as man sees; for man looks at the outward appearance, but the LORD looks at the heart."* He's not the one move on.

Do you see the importance of not allowing people to count you out? The Lord has the final say. Seven of Jesse's sons passed before Samuel but none were fit to be the next King. They were not the Lord's choice. Sons and daughters of the King, just when they counted you out, God spoke up on your behalf, "well Jesse are these all your sons?" Jesse replied, "no, there remains yet the youngest; there he is keeping the sheep." Get him and the Lord said, *"Arise, anoint him for he is the one!"* Just when they have counted you out the Lord speaks up on your behalf and anoints you in the midst of the people. Always remember there is a greater plan for your life. There was a call out for David, and there was something else in David that the Lord needed. David was living in the light of what he was given to do, then when it was time for him to be elevated, all he had to do was to walk in it. Likewise you must simply walk in the light. Do not allow the thoughts, words or actions of others to cause you to miss what God has for you. Refuse to believe the lies of the devil. He is a liar; he is the father of lies.

I'm sure they had counted David out, thinking he just keeps sheep. What does he know? There is nothing in him that resembles a king. They did not even call him in when Samuel arrived to anoint the next king. You see when there's a call out for you, God will see to it that YOU receive it. He has not forgotten you. He knows exactly where you are and what you are doing. His call can reach you no matter where you are in life. If the call reached David while tending the sheep, minding his own business, surely your call will reach you. No matter where you are in life regardless of your bad choices and negative attitude, surely God can reach you as well. There was a need for the greatness that was on the inside of David, he was a vessel of honor.

Are you ready to walk in your next place for God? In God's timing He will call you to more. Will you be ready? Will you be properly prepared? *"[16] I delight in your decrees; I will not neglect your word" (Psalm 119:16, NIV).* In order to properly prepare do not neglect the word. For *"[73] Your hands made me and formed me give me understanding to learn your commands" (Psalm 119:73, NIV).* Because He made you, He can give you understanding to learn the word. *"[96] To all perfection I see a limit; but your commands are boundless"(Psalm 119:96, NIV).* There is no limit to God. Do not allow anyone to limit your life in the Lord.

You see Samuel looked upon Eliab and thought he was the one but he was mistaken. Don't accept limitations of man because of outward appearances, like how you dress, how you talk, and how you walk. Don't allow them to size you up making you think you don't have what it takes to get the job or that you are not cute or thin enough. Don't accept their limits. These are the things that man will tell you but God can work through unusual circumstances, He works through your mess to turn it into a mountain of opportunity. God has placed treasures on the inside of you; do not feed on the lies of the enemy. God wants to use what He has placed on the inside of you. *"[96] To all perfection I see a limit; but your commands are boundless" (Psalm 119:96, NIV).* You have been refused by man but accepted by God. His commands are boundless! Despite all that you have experienced thus far, don't allow foolishness to cause you to die and go to hell. Let go of foolishness and walk according to God's word, seek Him with all your heart. Let it go and realize that against all odds, unusual circumstances, being counted out by family and friends, God has counted you in. The Lord is saying arise, anoint (insert your name) for he/she is the one.

> Now walk in the light, *"5 This is the message we have heard from him and declare to you, that God is light and in him is **no darkness at all**. 6 If we say that we have fellowship with him and walk in darkness, we lie and do not practice the truth. 7 But if we walk in the light, as He is in the light, we have fellowship with one another, and the blood of Jesus his Son cleanses us from all sin" (1 John 1:5-7, NKJV).*

As you accept the call of salvation or the ministry that God has placed on the inside of you, you must understand that God is light and in Him there is no darkness. In Him there is no sin, no conniving, confusion, backbiting, gossiping, lying, cheating or stealing. There are no illicit sexual activities, for in Him there is light. If you are practicing these things you are walking in darkness, you are not living according to the **truth**. Sons and daughters of the King one cannot remain in darkness and think they are in fellowship with the Lord. Walking in darkness and sin is walking contrary to the word of the Lord. *But if we walk in the light, as He is light, we have fellowship with one another, and the blood of Jesus his Son cleanses us from all sin.* When a Christian walks in the light as He is light we can have true fellowship with one another because our lifestyle will reflect that of Christ. And not only will we have true fellowship with one another but we can be cleansed from sin. Sons and daughters of the King as you continue to walk in God's light, the truth of His word, you will be all that He has called you to be. You will be able to do what He has equipped you to do. You must make the decision to walk in the light and not darkness. I encourage you to walk in God's light.

> *"¹ Blessed are they whose ways are blameless, who walk according to the law of the Lord. ² Blessed are they who keep his statues and seek him with all their heart" (Psalm 119:1-2, NIV).*

> *"¹⁰ Hear, my son, and receive my sayings, and the years of your life will be many. ¹¹ I have taught you in the way of wisdom; I have led you in right paths. ¹² When you walk, your steps will not be hindered. And when you run, you will not stumble. ¹³ Take firm hold of instruction, do not let go; keep her, for she is your life. ¹⁴ Do not enter the path of the wicked, and do not walk in the way of evil. ¹⁵ Avoid it, do not travel on it; turn away from it and pass on" (Proverbs 4:10-15, NKJV).*

You need to receive the instructions of the Lord. Be careful what path you take, for He has given you instructions for life. Whose instructions will you follow from this day forward? You have a choice to make, and I encourage you to answer the call and walk in the light.

INSIGHT AND REVELATION

Walking in the Light—*"Responding to the Call"*

*"¹ My little children, these things I write to you, so that you may not sin. And if anyone sins, we have an Advocate with the Father, Jesus Christ the righteous. ² And He Himself is the propitiation for our sins, and not **for ours only but also for the whole world**"* (1John 2:1-2, NKJV). God gave us His word so that we may not sin. But if you do sin, remember you have an Advocate with the Father, Jesus Christ who can help on your behalf. He died for our sins and because of His death you have been forgiven. Always keep a repentant heart. One that is ready to repent of all wrong doing. *"¹¹ Return now every one from his evil way, and make your ways and your doings good"* (Jeremiah 18:11, NIV).

"³Now by this we know that we know Him if we keep His commandments. ⁴ He who says, 'I know Him,' and does not keep His commandments, is a liar, and the truth is not in him. ⁵ But whoever keeps His word, truly the love of God is perfected in him. By this we know we are in Him. ⁶ He who says he abides in Him ought himself also to walk just as He walked" (1 John 2: 3-6, NKJV).

If you know Christ, are you keeping his commandments? Are you being truthful to yourself? The one who says they know Him but fails to keep His word is a liar and the "truth" is not in him. The one who keeps His word, the love of God is perfected in him and he is growing in maturity, walking just as Jesus walked. During Jesus earthly ministry *"⁴⁰ He grew and became strong in spirit, filled with wisdom and the grace of God was upon Him"* (Luke 2:40, NKJV). As you grow you shall be strong in spirit and filled with wisdom as well.

I HAVE MADE A COMMITMENT:

Lord I commit my mind to thee, so devil you have to flee.
Lord I commit my heart to thee, so devil you cannot change me.
Lord I commit my actions and speech to thee, so devil you just as well set me free.
Lord all that I say or do from this day forward, I commit it all unto thee.
I will be committed in my learning and my speech, I will be committed in all that I say and do!

The Lord is aware of those who are committed and those who are not. *"¹⁹ You are great in counsel and mighty in work, for Your eyes are open to all the ways of the sons of men, to give everyone according to his ways and according to the fruit of his doings. ²³ Am I a God near at hand, says the Lord, and not a God afar off? ²⁴ Can anyone hide himself in secret places, so I shall not see him? Says the Lord; do I not fill heaven and earth? Says the Lord"*(Jeremiah 32:19; 23:23-24, NKJV). What have you committed to do for the Lord?

Insight: The things that the spirit reveals to you at this point are very important to the making of a beautiful vessel. *"⁶ As you therefore have received Christ Jesus the Lord, so walk in Him,⁷ rooted and built up in Him and established in the faith, as you have been taught, abounding in it with thanksgiving" (Colossians 2:6-7, NKJV).*

TALK BACK:
Revelation: In your own words tell what the Lord revealed to you in this chapter.

_____
_____
_____
_____
_____
_____
_____
_____
_____
_____
_____
_____
_____
_____
_____
_____
_____
_____
_____
_____
_____
_____
_____
_____
_____
_____
_____
_____
_____
_____
_____
_____
_____
_____
_____

Chapter 5

Trust God for More

"⁷ Some trust in chariots, and some in horses; but we will remember the name of the Lord our God. ⁸ They have bowed down and fallen; but we have risen and stand upright" (Psalm 20:7-8, NKJV).

¹**Trust:** to depend or to rely. To be confident, to hope, something committed to the care of another.

Do you trust God for more? Regardless of where you are right now, do you trust God for more? God is well able to provide for your every need. Do you desire more? In whom do you trust? In Psalm 20:7 some trusted in chariots and horses, which were used in the battlefield. Will you likewise trust in things versus the name of the Lord our God who owns the very battle you are faced with? He has the means to supply you with what you need to be victorious in battle. Let us stop trusting in things, tools and people. You must learn to trust in God. In Psalm 20:8, those who trusted in things, tools, chariots and horses bowed down and fell. But those who trusted in the Lord our God rose and stood upright. He has all power to defeat the enemy. Will you trust God for more?

For some trust is a five-letter word that does not come easily. We often find ourselves putting our trust in people, whereas God desires for you to trust in Him to meet your needs. *"²⁸ In Him we live and move and have our being"* (Acts 17:28, NKJV).

"²⁶ He has made from one blood every nation of men to dwell on all the face of the earth and has determined their preappointed times and the boundaries of their dwellings. ²⁷ So they should seek the Lord, in the hope that they might grope for Him and find Him, though He is not far from each of us" (Acts 17:26-27, NKJV).

God created each of you from one blood to be on the earth. Not only did He create you but He has also determined your preappointed times and the boundaries of your dwelling. God has a purpose for your life and you must trust Him to bring it to pass.

"³⁰ . . . He is able to do exceedingly, abundantly, above all that we ask or think, according to the power that works in us . . ." (Ephesians 3:20, NKJV). We need His power to work in us. Will you trust God for more? Allow the Spirit of God to be loosed in you. You need to allow His spirit and nature to be free in you. Although His spirit is abiding within you, one can still be bound and consumed by the cares of this life, simply because they fail to trust God. Will you allow His spirit to be loosed in you and trust Him for more? When His spirit is loosed in you and you are being obedient to the word of God, you will no longer be hidden; people will recognize you and the ministry within you.

When Christ's spirit is loosed in you, things change, and circumstances change. You cannot be in the presence of an awesome God and walk away the same. If you find yourself in a place where your mind is agitated, confused, or in a nonproductive state then allow the spirit of God to be loosed in you. Trust God for more for He is able to do exceedingly, abundantly, above all that you ask or think. God is able to go beyond the limits of your thinking, He has unlimited power and authority over the entire universe. You serve a great God! He is able to break the power of Satan over the lives of people and He can do this according to the power that is working in you. So on today, will you allow the spirit of God to be SET FREE IN YOU! Will you trust God for more? Let Him loose in you!

"¹¹ . . . There was a woman who had a spirit of infirmity for eighteen years and was bent over and could in no way raise herself up. ¹² But when Jesus saw her, He called her to Him and said to her, "Woman, you are loosed from your infirmity." ¹³ And He laid His hands on her, and immediately she was made straight, and glorified God" (Luke 13: 11-13, NKJV). Jesus saw her, His divine inspection saw her condition and He reached out and laid His hands on her and immediately she was made straight. This woman was bound for eighteen years, but when Jesus spoke into her hearing, "Woman, you are loosed from your infirmity," a change took place. You need to know that Jesus sees your condition and a change will take place.

Sometimes in life you have circumstances and conditions that have caused you to be bent over in darkness, you are bowed and bent downward towards lower things. Now you find yourself unable to lift yourself up. I speak to your spirit to be loosed of your condition (sin) that has come to hinder you and to keep you distracted. Be loosed of those things that cause you to focus on stuff versus ministry. I speak to those things that keep you running away from God. I speak to your SPIRIT TO BE LOOSED in the name of JESUS! Satan I bind the spirit that has been launched out to attack (Insert your name). On this day I decree and declare that you will be all that God has called you to be. You will arise and trust God for more. No longer will you struggle with doing what is right, you shall be free in every area of your life. You need to know that God has already determined your preappointed times and the boundaries of your dwelling. You shall follow His plans for your life, in Jesus name. Amen.

Esther had to follow the plan of God as she trusted Him for more. No matter how many sought the title to be the next queen, it had already been determined and preappointed for her.

"² . . . Let beautiful young virgins be sought for the king. ³ . . . Let the beauty preparation be given to them. ⁴ Then let the young woman who pleases the king be queen instead of Vashti." ¹⁶Esther was taken to King Ahasuerus, into his royal palace. ¹⁷ . . . The king loved Esther more than all the other women, and she obtained grace and favor in his sight more than all the virgins; so he set the royal crown upon her head and made her queen instead of Vashti" (Esther 2:2-4,16-17 NKJV).

The plan God had for Esther came to pass. It was preappointed for her to be the next queen. You must grab this revelation for your life. Trust God for more, He has already determined your preappointed times. What are you worried about? It has already been preappointed. Why are you wrestling and struggling?

34

Can you trust God for more? *"²⁰ . . . He is able to do exceedingly, abundantly, above all that we ask or think, according to the power that works in us" (Ephesians 3:20, NKJV).* From this point forward no longer will you trust in things or people in an attempt to win. Trust God for more; He has your outcome in Him, for He is able to do all things. Trusting in chariots, horses, things, and people will cause you to bow and fall; but as you trust in the Lord you shall remain standing for you have been predestined for purpose.

Mary had to trust in God for what was about to happen in her life. *"²⁶ Now in the sixth month the angel Gabriel was sent by God to a city of Galilee named Nazareth, ²⁷ to a virgin betrothed to a man whose name was Joseph, of the house of David. The virgin's name was Mary. ²⁸ And having come in, the angel said to her, "Rejoice, highly favored one, the Lord is with you; blessed are you among women" ²⁹ But when she saw him, she was troubled at his saying, and considered what manner of greeting this was. ³⁰ Then the angel said to her, "Do not be afraid, Mary, for you have found favor with God. ³¹ And behold, you will conceive in your womb and bring forth a Son, and shall call His name Jesus. ³² He will be great, and will be called the Son of the Highest; and the Lord God will give Him the throne of His father David" (Luke 1:26-32, NKVJ).* Mary received a visit from the angel Gabriel telling her of things to come, which had been determined and preappointed. She did not understand and *"³⁴ Then Mary said to the angel, "How can this be, since I do not know a man?" ³⁵ And the angel answered and said to her, "The Holy Spirit will come upon you, and the power of the Highest will overshadow you; therefore, also, that Holy One who is to be born will be called the Son of God. ³⁸ Then Mary said, "Behold the maidservant of the Lord! Let it be to me according to your word." And the angel departed from her" (Luke 1:34, 35, 38, NKJV).* The angel told Mary what was going to take place, the things that had been determined and preappointed for Mary's life. Even though Mary could not understand it fully, she said, **"Let it be to me according to your word."** Mary was overshadowed by the power of God. When one is overshadowed by the power of God it takes over and completes its mission, a change occurs.

The spirit of God took over and allowed Mary to become pregnant. It was all preappointed, it had already been determined for Mary to give birth to Jesus. Mary had to let go of her understanding and release herself to God. She trusted Him for what He was doing in her life. Mary had to release herself to receive more. Will you allow God's spirit to overshadow you and receive more? You must make a decision, either you will or you will not trust God. Either you will or will not allow God to lead and guide your steps. From this day forward who will you trust? Make the decision today so you can move forward in life. Trust God for more!

INSIGHT AND REVELATION

Trust God for More

Do you desire to be in a different place with God? If so, what are doing to advance to the next place? There can be no advancement while being complacent. Stop complaining about your job, family, relationship, marriage, finances, and grades if you are not going to do anything to advance. If you desire to go beyond where you are today there is a requirement for you to do something different.

Prayer:

Lord I stand before you on this day, because I desire to advance to another place in you. I give you my all as I go to that new place in you. I surrender myself totally and completely to you. I will not breakdown but I will break through because I am trusting God for more. Let the blood of Jesus remove any unprogressive label from my life, any item of hindrance, I apply Jesus blood to my mind. I am advancing, I am growing, and I am moving forward in God, in Jesus name. Amen.

"28 Have you not known? Have you not heard? The everlasting God, the Lord, the Creator of the ends of the earth, neither faints nor is weary. His understanding is unsearchable. 29 He gives power to the weak and to those who have no might. He increases strength" (Isaiah 40:28-29, NKJV). You have to release yourself and trust God for more, He has what you need.

My Child Look up and Trust Me

When you are depressed or sad, look up and trust God
When you are hurting and confused, look up and trust God
When you are lonely and going through, look up and trust God
Trust Him for He will never lead you astray.

"24 Be of good courage, and He shall strengthen your heart, all you who hope in the Lord" (Psalm 31:24, NKJV).

Insight: The things that the spirit reveals to you at this point are very important to the making of a beautiful vessel. *"10 Those who know Your name will put their trust in You, for You, Lord, have not forsaken those who seek You" (Psalm 9:10, NKJV).* While writing this book a friend was editing this chapter and as she began reading she realized that she was bound, she had a brush of reality. She was going through some issues at work and needed to be loosed, there was a need to be free. So she scheduled a meeting with her department regarding the issues. In doing so, she began to pray that God would touch their hearts and they would not leave the meeting without solutions to the problems. Because she allowed God's spirit to be loosed in the situation, a change came, answers came, solutions were made and she was thankful for God's spirit being loosed, the meeting went great! Instead of using your voice to whine and complain, ask God to freely move in your situation. Just ask God for His help so you can be free.

TALK BACK:
Revelation: In your own words tell what the Lord revealed to you in this chapter.

Chapter 6

Despite the Process Triumph in Christ

When you hear the word process, what comes to your mind? A [1]**process** is a series of actions, changes or functions that achieve an end or result. It is something that happens over a series of time, it does not happen all at once.

When God created you in your mother's womb you were not the person you are today. You went through a process to become you. Whether great or small it still took time for you to develop. For instance, before you were a man (woman), you were a boy (girl); and before you were a boy (girl), you were a baby boy (girl); and before you were a baby boy (girl), you were a thought in the mind of God. And during the process of your life you've made some decisions some good and some not so good. But as you think about the decisions you've made and the things you've experienced what comes to your mind? What is your view of your life from where you are sitting today? When God created you in the form of a seed, He had a vision in mind.

- *You were created In His Image. (Reference Genesis 1:27)*
- *You Are Fearfully And Wonderful Made. (Reference Psalm 139:14)*
- *You Are Anointed. (Reference Psalm 20:6)*
- *You Are The Apple Of His Eye. (Reference Deuteronomy 32:10)*
- *You Are Healed. (Reference 1 Peter 2:24, Matthew 8:16-17)*
- *You Have Been Given The Shield Of Faith, And It Stops The Enemy. (Reference Ephesians 6:16)*
- *Satan Has No Power Over You. (Reference Romans 12:21)*
- *You Have Unlimited Protection. (Reference Psalm 91)*
- *You Are An Overcomer. (Reference 1 John 4:4, John 16:33)*
- *You Are Victorious.(Reference Romans 8:38, 2 Corinthians 2:14)*
- *You Are More Than A Conqueror. (Reference Romans 8:37)*
- *You Are Equipped to triumph in Him. (Reference 2 Corinthians 2:14)*

God is in the process of making you into a great and mighty vessel. Refuse to be fearful of the enemy who has arisen to attack your body but yet cannot kill your soul. I know you have experienced rejection, heartache, pain, loneliness, guilt, and shame but do not allow those things to cause you to fear the devil. Even though he seeks someone to devour you must stand firm against him as he launches his attack. "[7] *Submit to God, resist the devil and he will flee from you" (James 4:7, NKJV)*. It is easy to say what you must do when the devil launches his attack, but it may not be so easy to carry out. James first tells you to submit, in other words surrender, and yield to the will of God. Next He tells you to resist, to actively oppose with force, to stand against the devil and he will flee and vanish, giving you the victory.

Sons and daughters of the King *³¹ . . . Satan has asked for you, that he may sift you as wheat. ³² But the Lord has prayed for you, that your faith should not fail . . ."* (Luke 22:31-32, NKJV).

²Sift: to harass till nothing but chaff remains. It separates the good from the bad.

The process of sifting wheat is for the purpose of separating the wheat from the chaff, the good from the bad. Sifting wheat is accomplished by throwing the wheat into the air and allowing the chaff to be blown away, leaving just grain. Then the farmer prepares that which is profitable for the market. In your life God allows Satan to toss you to and fro for a time of sifting and to rid you of the mess in your heart. The devil desires to destroy you, but God has another plan for the sifting. He allows it to make you better, to shake you and to reveal the stuff you allowed to rest in your heart. *"You meant it for evil but God meant if for good" (Genesis 5:20, NKJV).* Despite the process you can triumph!

"²⁸ Do not fear those who kill the body but cannot kill the soul. But rather fear him who is able to destroy both soul and body in hell. ²⁹ Are not two sparrows sold for a copper coin? And not one of them falls to the ground apart from your father's will. ³⁰ But the very hairs on your head are all numbered. ³¹Do not fear therefore; you are more valuable than many sparrows" (Matthew 10:28-31, NKJV).

Stop looking at the things that the devil presents, do not fear him. Instead fear God for He is able to destroy both soul and body in hell. Do not allow how you feel to stop what God is doing in you. If He takes great care of the sparrow how much more will He do for you? *"²⁹Are not two sparrows sold for a copper coin? And not one of them falls to the ground apart from your father's will" (Matthew 10:29, NKJV).* Not one of them, no harm can be done to the sparrows apart from the father's will. Likewise, no harm can be done to you apart from the father's will. So whatever you may be facing in your life God is keenly aware of your situation. Nothing happens apart from His will, and it will not destroy you.

"¹ O Lord, You have searched me and know me. ²You know my sitting down and my rising up; You understand my thought afar off. ³ You comprehend my path and my lying down, and are acquainted with all my ways. ⁴For there is not a word on my tongue, but behold, O Lord, You know it altogether. ⁵ You have hedged me behind and before, and laid Your hand upon me" (Psalm 139:1-5, NKJV). God is active in your life. He is well acquainted with all your ways and the fruit of your lips. He has given you unlimited protection by placing a hedge around you. He has enclosed you, to protect you from the wiles of the devil. God is very powerful and He is concerned about you, He has formed a hedge around you and it causes the enemy to scatter. *"¹ Let God arise, let his enemies be scattered; let those who hate him flee before him" (Psalm 68:1, NKVJ).* This was a call for God's presence to be in effect in the lives of His enemies and those who hate Him. I speak to you now, let God arise in your life; allow Him to scatter your enemies. When He arise in your situation, your enemies shall scatter, they shall flee!

You don't have to toil or struggle any longer. God has complete control, *"¹⁰ Be strong in the Lord and in the power of His might" (Ephesians 6:10, NKJV). "¹⁷ No weapon formed against you shall prosper (Isaiah 54:17, NKJV).* [18] *And I also say to you that you are Peter, and on this rock I will build My church, and the gates of Hades shall not prevail against it"* (Matthew 16:18, NKJV). I bind and destroy every spirit that has attacked you to rob you of your blessings, in Jesus Name, you shall triumph in Christ?

> *"[14] God always leads us in triumph in Christ and through us diffuses the fragrance of His knowledge in every place. [15] For we are to God the fragrance of Christ among those that are being saved and among those who are perishing. [16] To the one we are the aroma of death leading to death; to the other the aroma of life leading to life. And who is sufficient for these things"* (2 Corinthians 2:14-16, NKJV).

[3]**Triump:** to have victory over something, to win, to succeed.
[4]**Diffuse:** to pour out and cause to spread freely, to scatter or spread about, to soften.

No matter what is going on in your life, God will lead you to triumph in Christ. You will have the victory over life circumstances. No longer will you lie dormant before your enemy allowing him to run rampant in your life. He will give you a measure of knowledge to combat all attacks.

You have His fragrance of power, dominion, and victory which allows you to release his aroma over different areas in your life and the life of others. In order to walk in victory over your circumstance you must obey the word of God and maintain His knowledge. Now as you call Jesus He will answer you. *Jeremiah 33:3 "Call unto me and I will answer you and show you great and mighty things, which you do not know" (NKJV).* Whatever need you may have call Jesus and He will answer; He will cause you to triumph in Christ. Knowing this, from this point forward I encourage you to call Jesus. Refuse to go backward, despite the process, triumph in Christ. Don't allow circumstances or people to cause you to go back. You can't afford to go back. After the crossing of the Red Sea miracle the children of Israel were in the wilderness whining and complaining about why they were in this place? They said, "We should have stayed in Egypt." Never mistake obstacles, roadblocks, closed doors or pain as a reason to turn back. Remain focused and call on Jesus. Refuse to allow what you don't understand to block or kill your dreams. At this point in your life you must move forward for God has great things for you and you shall be that beautiful vessel of honor.

> *"[7] Rest in the Lord, and wait patiently for Him, do not fret because of him who prospers in his way, because of the man who brings wicked schemes to pass.*
>
> *[34] Wait on the Lord and keep His way, and He shall exalt you to inherit the land . . ."* (Psalm 37:7, 34, NKJV).

Wait I say on the Lord, remain in a state of readiness of expectation for Him. Do not seek answers from others, God has your answer. Do not allow others to change your course of direction. Know who you are following. You can't afford to follow any path. God has a set path just for you. So *"[10] Be strong in the Lord and the power of his might" (Ephesians 6:10, NKJV).* Satan is waiting for the opportune time to come and try your faith. Just as he tempted Jesus when He had fasted for forty days in the wilderness He likewise will tempt you. According to *Luke 4:13 "When the devil had ended every temptation, he departed from him until his opportune time" (NKJV).* The devil was waiting on a time that was suited for a particular purpose, a more favorable or fitting time in which one would not expect the attack. Despite the attacks, tricks, and schemes of the devil, be determined that you will triumph in Christ. Call on Jesus and He will show you great and mighty things which you do not know. Call Jesus!

INSIGHT AND REVELATION

Despite the Process Triumph in Christ

I Will Grow

Inspite of what's before me, I will grow.
No matter who opposes me, I will grow.
Even though my enemies and foes come to devour me, I will grow.
No matter how much pain I have experienced or am presently experiencing, I will grow.
So inspite of my trials, persecution, heartache, mishaps, shortcomings, or failures; I will grow.

I will be obedient to the call, I will grow.
I will rise above the fall, I will grow.
I will strive to do my best in everything that I do, I will grow.
I will do it with a hint of excellence and it shall reach you no matter where you go, I will grow.

Insight: The things that the spirit reveals to you at this point are very important to the making of a beautiful vessel. *"24 Jesus said to his disciples, if any one would come after me, let him deny himself and take up his cross and follow me" (Matthew 16:24, NKJV).*

TALK BACK:
Revelation: In your own words tell what the Lord revealed to you in this chapter.

_____
_____
_____
_____
_____
_____
_____
_____
_____
_____
_____
_____

SECTION III

REFUSE TO BE DETAINED:

This section deals with building upon your

foundation, becoming a beautiful vessel.

Chapter 7

Stop Mourning and Live

"Press on"

Are you tired of difficulties and wavering in your life? Are you ready to live the life that God has so richly promised? Then I encourage you to stop mourning and live. David said in *Psalm 30:11 "You have turned my mourning into dancing; You have put off my sackcloth and clothed me with gladness" (NKJV). "¹¹ You changed my mourning into dancing. You took off my funeral clothes and dressed me up in joy" (Psalm 30:11, CEB).* The Lord transformed David's situation. Instead of mourning, David danced; the Lord removed his old garments, his funeral clothes and clothed him with the spirit of joy and gladness. He gave him an exchange in the midst of darkness and despair, he changed his disposition. David was up on his feet rejoicing! Will you allow the Lord to give you an exchange on today, regardless of what you have lost? He is able to restore and revive your situation. You too will be up on your feet rejoicing! Never give up on life because of losses and failures. Rely on God and He will make the exchange. He will turn your sadness into joy. It may be traumatic and chaotic right now, but be willing to make the exchange, get up and live—press on.

How long do you intend to mourn over your situation? You cannot continue to allow your circumstances to control you. Stop mourning and live, you must press on. When one is faced with a lifeless situation, they tend to allow it to rest heavily upon their heart, causing them to be frustrated and anxious. Stress then sneaks in and attacks their body, leading to other aliments. You can not keep allowing your nonproductive situation to destroy you. Release it to the Lord and press on, knowing that *"⁵ Those who sow in tears shall reap in joy" (Psalm 126:5, NKJV).* You need to understand its reaping time, now receive your joy. Devil your time is up, no longer will I allow you to hold me in captivity. It is imperative that you move from that place, you have to get up and live for your days of mourning are over. No more feeding the dead situation, you must press on.

David mourned over his son Absalom who sought to take his kingdom. Absalom began to steal the hearts of the men of Israel. As they were going to see King David for judgment, Absalom stopped them before they reached the king and settled the matter. Therefore, the people's hearts were turned to Absalom instead of David and the conspiracy grew strong, for the people with Absalom continually increased in number (2 Samuel Ch. 15).

¹³Now a messenger came to David, saying, "The hearts of the men of Israel are with Absalom." ¹⁴So David said to all his servants who were with him at Jerusalem, "Arise, and let us flee, or we shall not escape from Absalom . . ." (2 Samuel 15:13-14, NKJV).

Because of Absalom's conspiracy against his father they were preparing to go to battle against each other. David told his warriors not to hurt Absalom even though he was doing this wicked deed. He said, *[5]" 'Deal gently for my sake with the young man Absalom.' And all the people heard when the king gave all the captains orders concerning Absalom. So the people went out into field of battle against Israel." [9]Then Absalom met the servants of David. Absalom rode on a mule and the mule went under the thick boughs of a great terebinth tree and his head caught in the terebinth; so he was left hanging between heaven and earth. And the mule which was under him went on. [10]Now a certain man saw it and told Joab. [14]Joab took three spears in his hand and thrust them through Absalom's heart. While he was still alive in the midst of the terebinth tree. [10]And ten young men that bore Joab's armor surrounded Absalom, and struck and killed him. [17]And they took Absalom and cast him into a large pit in the woods, and laid a very large heap of stones over him. Then all of Israel fled everyone to his own tent" (2 Samuel 18: 5-6;9-17, NKJV).*

When David heard about the death of his son Absalom he mourned, *[33]The king was deeply moved and went up to his chamber over the gate and wept, he said, "O my son Absalom—my son, my son Absalom—if only I had died in your place! O Absalom my son, my Son" (2 Samuel 18:33, NKJV)!*

[1] And Joab was told, "Behold, the king is weeping and mourning for Absalom. [2] So the victory that day was turned into mourning for all the people. For the people heard it said that day, "The King is grieved for his son." [4] The king covered his face and cried out with a loud voice, O my son Absalom! O Absalom, my son, my son" (2 Samuel 19:1, 2, 4 NKJV)!

We see that as Absalom went out for battle while riding his mule his head got caught in the terebinth tree and it left him hanging in mid air without his armor, he was alone. The enemy was caught in mid air with no one around to help him. God is able to allow your enemy to hang himself; He can give the enemy over unto you. Joab and his men then killed Absalom and threw his body in a pit; this caused the men of Israel to flee back to their tent and they did not continue to battle. However, when David heard about his son's death, instead of rejoicing over the victory, he was mourning. He was hurt, and he grieved for his son. The pain was deep, he cried out for his son, his loss. Have you ever been in a place where on one side you felt you should rejoice, but on the other side you were mourning the loss? Then understand and know that it is time for you to make the exchange. Will you accept the exchange to turn your mourning into dancing?

*"[5] Then Joab came into the house to the king, and said, "Today you have disgraced all your servants who today have saved your life, the lives of your sons and daughters, the lives of your wives and the lives of your concubines, [6] in that you love your enemies and hate your friends. For you have declared today that you regard neither princes nor servants; for today I perceive that if Absalom had lived and all of us had died today, then it would have pleased you well. [7] **Now therefore, arise, go out and speak comfort to your servants.** For I swear by the Lord, if you do not go out, not one will stay with you this night. And that will be worse for you than all the evil that has befallen you from your youth until now." [8] Then the king arose and sat in the gate. And they told all the people, saying, "There is the king, sitting in the gate." So all the people came before the king" (2 Samuel 19: 5-8, NKJV).*

David had to make the exchange, he had to rise up and live. Even though his son was dead, he was their enemy, and he should not continue to mourn over the enemy. You must get up and live! David had to encourage his troops; he had to speak into their lives, for truly it was their day of victory. He had to stop mourning and press on.

Many of you have suffered much. You have experienced a great loss but I speak to you now in the name of Jesus, get up and live. You do not have to remain in this place, you can make the exchange. David could not remain in a state of mourning, but he had to get up and encourage his troops because they still had battles to fight. If David had remained in his state of mourning what would have happened to his city, his family and his troops? If you remain in your state of mourning what will happen to you and your family?

Despite your barren situation (s) and the years you've had to endure, it's time to make the exchange and live more abundantly. Inspite of all the broken promises, the heartache, and pain you have experienced, make the exchange and live more abundantly. Inspite of the enemy rising against you, stop mourning and live life more abundantly. Walk in your "overflow," your "abundance." Press on!

"¹²Not that I have already attained, or am already perfected; but I press on, that I may lay hold of that for which Christ Jesus has also laid hold of me. ¹³Brethren, I do not count myself to have apprehended; but one thing I do, forgetting those things which are behind and reaching forward to those things which are ahead, ¹⁴ I press toward the goal for the prize of the upward call of God in Christ Jesus" *(Philippians 3:12-14, NKJV).*

Sons and daughters of the king, you must press on, forgetting those things which are behind and reaching forward to those things which are ahead. Don't allow your past to stop you from reaching your potential for your future. Obtain your prize, move forward.

In the hustle and bustle of life when it seems most chaotic, what is one to do? When it gets to the point that it seems impossible to continue on, what is one to do? When life suddenly throws you a curve and moves you off your comfortable path, what is one to do? One must continue to press on. Forget those things which are behind and reach forward to those things which are ahead, its time to forget and move forward. God has great things ahead for you but in order to receive them you have to first forget those things which are behind. Let the past go, release yourself from the past. Release yourself from the pain and hurt. Release yourself from the loss and failure. It's time to let it go, turn the page and make the exchange. Press on and move forward.

You may have experienced numerous things over this past year, but even in all the events you must realize there is hope for a brighter future. Continue to press onward for the prize of that which lies above, the prize that no other can give unto you. *"⁶Be strong and of good courage, do not fear nor be afraid . . ."* *(Deuteronomy 31:6, NKJV).*

In times when the cares of life begin to arise more frequently and it seems overwhelming, when you think it's over and there is no hope, what shall you do? Be strong and of good courage, do not fear nor be afraid, the Lord is with thee. Lift your hands in total surrender, allowing the Lord to have total control. Press on; stand firm and steadfast on His word letting nothing separate you from His love.

Prayer:

> I choose to let go of all distractions, hurt, and pain. I am not running from the devil, for I am *"7 resisting the devil, and he is fleeing from me" (James 4:7, NKJV)*. For I realize I possess supernatural help in every situation, *"2 My help comes from the Lord, who made heaven and earth" (Psalm 121:2, NKJV)*. I am not stuck in my life but I am growing and moving and changing. I am free to grow in God. I am growing in Him everyday. *"36 Therefore if the Son sets you free you shall be FREE INDEED" (John 8:36, NKJV)!*

Thank You Jesus I am free:

- from pain of mourning, hurt and disappointment
- from negative reports and lifeless situations
- from fears, anxiety, stress and worry
- from all mental and emotional bondages (depression, oppression, grief, guilt and broken heartedness)
- from unforgiveness, bitterness, resentment and hatred
- from betrayal, rejection and envy
- from all spirits of infirmity, sickness and disease
- from spirits of death and suicide

I boldly declare that I am free! *I am an overcomer in every area of my life (reference Revelation 12:11, NKJV). I am more than a conqueror through Jesus Christ (reference Romans 8:37, NKJV). Whom the Son sets free is free indeed (Reference John 8:36, NKJV). Amen!*

Paul and Silas endured hard times in the book of Acts chapter 16. They had been beaten and were thrown into jail. Doors closed in their face, but yet they began to sing hymns and praise God. Through their pressing, by midnight, a change came; they were released, freed from jail, their opposing enemy did not win. Likewise as you continue to press forward, the enemy will not win. So continue to press on, press your way my child, just press. Make the exchange, stop mourning and live.

INSIGHT AND REVELATION

Stop Mourning and Live—*"Press on"*

Things may not always go in the direction that you like,
> but even in those times God is always present a shining light.

He said be still and follow my agenda,
    for He is always present standing right by your side.

Even though it may not feel good,
    and you may have to cry from time to time, continue to press on my child.

At times it might seem that it's unbearable and you can't seem to move on
    you must put your trust in Him and keep pressing on.

You may feel lonely and a little depressed
    but remember look not at your present state and press on my child.

You may be sick and tired of the chaos
    but do not worry, instead keep pressing on.

When your circumstances are pleasant, forget about the past and press on and when your circumstances are unbearable or feel degrading, forget about those things and press on.

God is going to turn your pressure into power, your test into a testimony. He is going to transform your trials into your triumphs. Stop mourning and press on. Your breakthrough is on the way. Position yourself for something great; lay aside every weight, hindrance and excuse. Press on!

Insight: The things that the spirit reveals to you at this point are very important to the making of a beautiful vessel. "³⁶ *You need to persevere so that when you have done the will of God, you will receive what he has promised" (Hebrews 10:36, NIV).*

TALK BACK: Revelation: In your own words tell what the Lord revealed to you in this chapter.

_____
_____
_____
_____
_____
_____
_____
_____
_____
_____
_____
_____
_____
_____
_____
_____

Chapter 8

Refuse to be Detained

"Get up and Let's Go"

"¹ Therefore, since we are surrounded by such a great cloud of witnesses, let us throw off everything that hinders and the sin that so easily entangles. And let us run with perseverance the race marked out for us" (Hebrews 12:1 NIV).

What have you allowed to entangle you, to stop you, to hinder you? Lay it aside, throw it off. Don't allow anything to detain you from moving and growing as a child of God.

Often times because of life's circumstances, you may find it hard to move forward in the things of God. Stop allowing things to trip you up, to keep you from moving forward. Refuse to remain in your holding pattern. Reveal unto me Lord, what I have allowed to rest in my heart that keeps tripping me up. Help me to deal with my issues. I realize I need your help, so as you reveal the true issues of my heart; I will lay them aside and give them to you. Today, will you lay it aside, throw it off, clear it out, and let it go so you can move forward and become the beautiful vessel of honor that He intended for you to be?

There is absolutely no way anyone or anything can detain, delay or keep you from proceeding, and producing. No matter what you are facing, God has a plan and a call for your life. Your ministry awaits and its time to get up and move forward. Let the body of Christ tell the devil no, no to his tricks, schemes, plans, and tactics. It stops here! It is time to get up and move forward. Do not waste any more time on things that you have deemed as important. Refuse to be detained any longer. You were created for a purpose, to reach a certain destination in life. As you reflect over your life, are you walking in line with God's word for your life?

"⁷But we have this treasure in earthen vessels, that the excellence of the power may be of God and not of us. ⁸We are hard-pressed on every side, yet not crushed; we are perplexed, but not in despair; ⁹perescuted, but not forsaken, struck down, but not destroyed . . ." (2 Corinthians 4:7-9, NKJV).

As an earthen vessel, God has given you power to overcome all circumstances. You may be hard pressed on every side, yet not crushed. Attacked from every angle, but not crushed into powder. You will not be trampled or oppressed severely to the point that it's going to destroy you. Numerous things can happen when one is hard pressed on every side, but even so, you are not crushed. You may even be perplexed, yet not in despair, or miserable, for this is not your disposition. You may be going through right now, but refuse to allow it to stop you from proceeding and producing. Don't allow it to detain you. God's word is the final word in your life, so get up and go, for your ministry awaits, you are predestined for purpose.

Persecution will come to harass and to cause oppression, don't allow it to settle in your heart. God has given you the ability to overcome persecution, He has promised to be with you. Once you allow oppression to settle in your heart its goal is to destroy you. Refuse to be detained by the spirit of oppression—get up! *"¹ You therefore my son be strong in the grace that is in Christ Jesus. ³You therefore must endure hardship as a good solider of Jesus Christ" (2 Timothy 2:1, 3 NKJV).*

You may get struck down, but it shall not destroy you. God allowed Satan to attack Job on every side and in every way and it was all for a purpose. He will allow Satan to attack you as well for a time and a purpose. *"¹Job was blameless and upright; he feared God and shunned evil" (Job 1:1 NKJV).* Even in this, it did not cause Satan to attack him less than others. God allowed Satan to attack him; Job was hard-pressed on every side, yet not crushed. He was perplexed, but not in despair. He was persecuted, but not forsaken; he was struck down, but not destroyed. *"The Lord said to Satan, "¹²Behold all that he has is in your power only do not lay a hand on his person" (Job 1:12 NKJV).* So Satan struck Job four times on every side in every way.

1. He took away his oxen, donkeys and killed the servants
2. Killed his sheep
3. Camels were taken
4. Killed sons and daughters

His final attack was on Job's body. Job endured hardship as a good solider of Jesus Christ. The Lord would not allow Satan to take his life. Job was indeed being attacked on every side, he said, *"⁸He had fenced up my way, so that I cannot pass and he has set darkness in my paths. ⁹He has stripped me of my glory, and taken the crown from my head. ¹⁰He breaks me down on every side, and I am gone; my hope he has uprooted like a tree" (Job 19:8-10 NKJV).*

Satan's goal was to destroy Job, but Job's response was:
*"²⁵**I know that my Redeemer lives**; and he shall stand at last on the earth; ²⁶ and after my skin is destroyed, this I know, that in my flesh I shall see God" (Job 19:25-26 NKJV).* Job was struck down, he lost a lot, but to God be the glory, he did not lose his mind, nor his heart to seek after other gods. He was not destroyed, Job said, ***I know that my Redeemer (My protector, my provider, my healer, my deliver) lives and I shall see him!***

Just at the right time, at the precise hour and the exact moment, God intervened and began to restore Job. Job's blessings had doubled compared to what he had in the beginning. God will not forsake you, He is the Most High King who super rules. He will surpass your plan to bring about something great in you. He has stamped his sign of approval on your situation and you must endure, hold on, *"²²Cast your burden on the Lord and He shall sustain (keep you); he shall never permit the righteous to be moved" (Psalm 55:22 NKJV). ²⁸For all things work together for the good of those who love the Lord" (Romans 8:28 NKJV).*

We must tell the devil the facts:
>*I am hard pressed on every side—yet not destroyed.*
>*I am perplexed—but not in despair.*
>*I am persecuted—but not forsaken.*
>*I am struck down—but not destroyed.*

In other words, realize what situation you are in and know that you might be hard pressed, perplexed, persecuted, struck down but yet, you must know that the devil can not destroy you. You are not lost for Jesus is on your side. He is your example to follow, He was hard pressed by many, persecuted, perplexed, struck down, but He did not allow any of it to stop his purpose or to detain him. So you must get up and do likewise, refuse to be detained, for you are predestined for purpose.

Jesus was one who was doing all the right things, but yet and still many stood before Him to persecute Him. It matters not if you've done wrong or not, Satan will use anyone he can to rise up against you. In the book of Exodus we see after the death of Joseph, a new king arose over Egypt who did not know Joseph. *"⁹And he said to his people, "Look, the people of the children of Israel are more and mightier than we; ¹⁰come, let us deal shrewdly with them, lest they multiply, and it happen, in the event of war, that they also join our enemies and fight against us, and so go up out of the land." ¹¹Therefore they set taskmasters over them to afflict them with their burdens. And they built for Pharaoh supply cities, Pithom and Raamses. ¹²But the more they afflicted them, the more they multiplied and grew. And they were in dread of the children of Israel. ¹³So the Egyptians made the children of Israel serve with rigor. ¹⁴And they made their lives bitter with hard bondage—in mortar, in brick, and in all manner of service in the field. All their service in which they made them serve was with rigor" (Exodus 1:9-14 NKJV).* They (Egyptian/King) were afraid of the children of Israel because they felt they were mightier. But our text shows that the more the Egyptians afflicted them, the more the children of Israel multiplied and grew. They did not allow their afflictions to stop them from producing life. Do you allow your afflictions to stop you from producing in your life? Have you allowed your afflictions to stunt or hinder your spiritual growth process? You must be like the children of Israel, regardless of their affliction they grew and multiplied. In what area (s) have you multiplied in since your affliction?

The enemy wanted to kill their seed so he could stop them from increasing. They (children of Israel) were seen as a threat to them, therefore, they did all they could to stop them from growing. As you plant your seed (word of God) on the inside of you it shall spring up and you shall be prepared for every good work, useful for the Lord. The devil will then try to attack in every area possible so that your seed (word of God) will not grow or produce a harvest. He does not want you to operate in your gifts that God has given you. He wants you to be ineffective in God's Kingdom. The devil will devise a plan against you so you will not operate in your gift. He is trying to stop God's ultimate plan and purpose for your life. How long will you allow the enemy to stop you? Child of God get up and let's go, there is work to be done. Refuse to be detained; God has predestined you for purpose.

No matter how long the children of Israel had to go through, it worked for their good and produced God's glory. It was an eternal thing God did within them; He strengthened them to endure and not to cave in. So when all hell breaks loose in your life, remember, don't lose heart, don't despair, don't give up, release it, let it go and move forward.

"¹⁸ Do not look at the things which are seen for the things which are seen are temporary, but the things which are not seen are eternal" (2 Corinthians 4:18, NKJV). It's time to shift your focus to that which is not seen, from temporary problems to the glorious eternal rewards you shall receive. Lord help us not to be self absorbed, help us to fix our eyes on things above. We realize the things in this world are temporary, but we anticipate something better: eternal joy, peace, and love. We refuse to allow flesh to dictate, or to have dominion and rank. As you continue to walk with God, refuse to doubt or entertain the devil and his schemes. Refuse to be detained any longer. Obey the word of God and you will succeed in allowing God's word to rule in your life. It is possible; you can do it! Refuse to be detained, get up and move forward.

> Get up from your messy lifestyle, foolish and idle thinking.
> Get up from that empty position with your do nothing mentality.
> Get up from thinking that you've got it together, stinky thinking.

This is a new season in your life and you need to get up and move forward. Now receive your divine instruction. I believe God is ready to release instructions to you. Are you prepared to listen? I declare from this day forward, you will not seek after your own will but the will of the Father. You will not whine, bicker or complain when ministry work has been placed before you; instead you shall complete it with a spirit of excellence. Learn to do God's work without complaining and grumbling, do it with joy. Do not allow your job to wither because you are wandering from place to place, grumbling from house to house, bickering from person to person, and complaining from day to day. Are you tired of living the same old way, doing the same old things, to find your harvest so few and in between? Jesus is available for you. Refuse to be detained; stop allowing your whining, complaining, bickering, and lying to stop you from reaching your destiny. Get up and let's go!

INSIGHT AND REVELATION

Refuse to be Detained—*"Get up and Let's Go"*

¹Locust: numerous grasshoppers traveling in swarms and causing damage to vegetation.

When you proclaim salvation there are things to be done but often people allow persecutions and circumstances to stunt their growth. In the book of *Joel chapter 1* it talks about how the land laid waste and *how what the chewing locust left, the swarming locust has eaten, and what the swarming locust left, the crawling locust has eaten, and what the crawling locust left, the consuming locust had eaten.* He was calling the people to awake for the land was destroyed. All trees of the field had withered; even their joy had withered due to the disaster in the land. Have you allowed your circumstance and persecutions to cause your joy to wither? Surely your land has not been destroyed? Even though the land was destroyed, Joel still cried out to the Lord. He was not in despair going around as if there was no hope or release; instead he sought the Lord for assistance. In the midst of disastrous times, who are you seeking?

Your heart is God's land that needs cultivating and different types of locust have come to devour. What is stealing your time in pursuing Jesus, causing your land to lay waste to be in a disastrous state? Was it the stealing locust, the lazy and unproductive locust, the gossiping and busybody locust or the I'm tired locust? What have you allowed to keep you detained? Since your heart is in need of cultivating, you must take the time to rid yourself of some things. It's time to release those locusts from your life that have caused great damage. Whether it is an abusive relationship or a destructive habit you must release it and let it go. Don't allow it to keep you detained in this location any longer. Think about your life and where you are today, God desires for you to be continually moving forward in Him. This is your day of restoration. All the hell you have experienced is now over. Lord release your perfect will in my life, restore my joy, my peace, and my love for others. Restore my relationships, my family, my children and my finances in Jesus name. The enemy is powerless and harmless; he will not win. This is a day of restoration and (insert your name) shall move forward in Jesus name. Amen.

Insight: The things that the spirit reveals to you at this point are very important to the making of a beautiful vessel. *"[15] Though he slay me, yet will I trust in him: but I will maintain mine own ways before him" (Job 13:15 KJV).*

TALK BACK:
Revelation: In your own words tell what the Lord revealed to you in this chapter.

_____
_____
_____
_____
_____
_____
_____
_____
_____
_____
_____
_____
_____
_____
_____
_____
_____
_____
_____

Chapter 9

Hold Your Head Up

"This is your Make up day"

Hold your head up no matter what you have done,
    hold your head up for you are God's chosen one.

Hold your head up for the new life you have just begun,
    hold your head up and acknowledge Christ as God's son.

Hold your head up and live your life for God
    abounding in his presence.

Hold your head up for you will surely win,
    hold your head up and dream like you have never dreamed.

Hold your head up and seize the opportunities,
    hold your head up, now kneel and bow before the king.

Hold your head up for God is well able to deliver,
    so hold your head up and run towards the King.

Hold your head up!

Understand this, sons and daughters of the Most High King, where you are standing now is not your end. God has something better for you, so hold your head up. Despite the promises you have broken and the pain you may be experiencing, there is more for you. All of the promises of God are yea and amen. God is in the process of making you over on today, this is your make up day, so hold your head up for something better is on the way.

> *"³ I went down to the potter's house, and there he was, making something at the wheel. ⁴ And the vessel that he made of clay was marred in the hand of the potter, so he made it again into another vessel, as it seemed good to the potter to make. ⁵ Then the word of the Lord came to me, saying: ⁶ O house of Israel, can I not do with you as this potter?" says the Lord. "Look, as the clay is in the potter's hand, so are you in My hand, O house of Israel" (Jeremiah 18:3-6 NKJV).*

Jesus is the potter and you are the clay. Today is your make up day. This is your start over day. This is your get up and go day. He's sitting at the wheel of your life and He's making good use of your mistakes, bad decisions, and empty promises for you have been predestined for purpose. Hold your head up, the Potter is at the wheel reshaping and molding you. He sees how you have allowed your potential to lie dormant; you are not using what He gave you. He sees how you continue to dwell in darkness of past hurt and failures. He sees your blemishes and shortcomings. But, it seems good to Him to make you over again. This is your makeup day in the spirit and you must avail yourself to the Potter, will you become marred in His hands, will you allow Him to operate the wheel of your life? Will you let Him make you over again? For it seemed good to Him to do this.

It's time to be real with yourself for the Potter; Jesus Christ is already aware of your every need. He's already sitting at the wheel of your life. He sees how His vessel made of clay is marred in His hand, so it seems good to Jesus to make you over into another vessel. You are that marred vessel, that has been damaged and bruised and He is sitting at the wheel ready to make you over. Take a few minutes to examine your life.

- Are you one who has been hard-headed and rebellious? Then make me over Lord.
- Have you been caught up in gossiping, lying, grumbling, and complaining about other people? Then make me over Lord.
- Are you lazy and slack in doing kingdom work? Then make me over Lord.
- Have you been hurt, feeling abandoned, unloved? Then make me over Lord.
- Have you experienced sickness in your body? Then make me over Lord.
- Have you refused to put Christ first in your life? Then make me over Lord.
- Have you allowed your mouth to be given over to sin? Then make me over Lord.
- Have you used manipulation to trick and deceive others? Then make me over Lord.
- Have you taken things that do not belong to you? Then make me over Lord.
- Have you given your body over to others knowing, that is not your spouse? Then make me over Lord.
- Have you tried drugs and abused your body? Then make me over Lord.
- Have you sought to drink or eat your problems away? Then make me over Lord.
- Have you led others into the street of sin? Then make me over Lord.

After a thorough examination of your life do you realize you need help? Will you be willing to allow the Lord to make you over? After perfect revelation about all the things you have practiced that is contrary to God's word are you ready to change? It does one absolutely no good to see their sin, faults, and failures and walk away doing nothing about it. What will you do on today with what have been revealed to you? Will you allow the Lord to cleanse you; will you sit at His wheel and allow Him to make you over? Being in Jesus' hand He sees you beyond where you are. He sees the need to make you over into another vessel; He has not given up on you. He did not cast you aside, but He saw the need to restore, to polish, and to make you anew. Will you accept?

If you are reading this book then know that Jesus does not intend for your life to end at your current state. He has more for you. He is your Potter, He sits at the wheel of your life shaping and molding you into the image that most reflects Him. He sees your condition and instead of talking about you, or saying hurtful words to you He sits at the wheel of your life, seeking to reshape and mold you over again. In order to be a pure, clean, and holy vessel He knows that you must release your way of doing things. So Christ continues to mold, shape and trim the essence of your heart into a vessel of honor. It's not over, hold your head up; this is your makeup day.

Being in the Potter's hand He will make you over again. What do you need for the Potter to make again in your life? Do you need to step out of emotional baggage, rejection or low self esteem, depression or loneliness, or a feeling of defeat? Will you allow Him to make you over? Defeated in your thinking, make us over Lord, defeated in your marriage and relationships, make us over Lord. Will you allow Him to put your marriage on the wheel? God put Hosea and Gomer's marriage on the Potter's wheel and while on this wheel He felt it best to make their marriage over again. He knows the power of restoration. Gomer was unfaithful in the marriage but Hosea kept on loving her. Hurt, heartache, and pain but he was on the wheel and he continued to love her as instructed by the Lord.

Their story goes like this: The marriage was called to be by the Lord. *"²When the Lord began to speak by Hosea, the Lord said to Hosea: "Go, take yourself a wife of harlotry and children of harlotry . . . ³So he went and took Gomer, the daughter of Dibliam and she conceived and bore him a son. ⁶And she conceived again and bore a daughter . . . ⁸ . . . She conceived and bore a son"* (Hosea 1:2, 3, 6, 8 NKJV). *"⁵For their mother has played the harlot; she who conceived them has behaved shamefully. For she said, I will go after my lovers, who give me my bread and my water, My wool and my linen, my oil and my drink"* (Hosea 2:5 NKJV). Hosea was told to marry a prostitute who already had children. In the midst of their marriage she bore two children and Hosea was not the father. The Lord knew what Gomer was prior to telling Hosea to marry her. She was a prostitute and she sought her lovers in a way that she should have been seeking her husband.

But because the Lord specializes in restoration He allowed the marriage to happen. Even in seeking her lovers the Lord did not give up on her, instead He put her on the wheel and began to deal with the issues that she cherished in her heart. *⁶Therefore, behold, I will hedge up your way with thorns, and wall her in, so that she cannot fine her paths. ⁷She will chase her lovers, but not overtake them; yes, she will seek them, but not find them. Then she will say,' I will go and return to my first husband, for then it was better for me than now.'⁸ For she did not know that I gave her grain, new wine, and oil, and multiplied her silver and gold—which they prepared for Baal. ⁹"Therefore I will return and take away my grain in its time and my new wine in its season, And will take back my wool and my linen, given to cover her nakedness. ¹⁰Now I will uncover her lewdness in the sight of her lovers, and no one shall deliver her from my hand.¹¹I will also cause all her mirth to cease, her feast days, her New Moons, her Sabbaths—All her appointed feasts. ¹²" And I will destroy her vines and her fig trees, of which she has said,' These are my wages that my lovers have given me.' So I will make them a forest, and the beasts of the field shall eat them. ¹³I will punish her for the days of the Baals to which she burned incense. She decked herself with her earrings and jewelry, and went after her lovers; but Me she forgot," says the* LORD. *(Hosea 2:6-13 NKJV).* While at this place the Lord had to strip Gomer of things. She desired her lovers and what they could give her. She refused to acknowledge the Lord and therefore He had to make her over again. In making her over she would return home to her first husband, for she was predestined for purpose. Even though she sought her lovers, God still had a plan for her life.

Not only did He give Gomer a make over He put Hosea on the wheel and He told Hosea, *"¹ . . . Go again, love a woman who is loved by a lover and is committing adultery, just like the love of the Lord for the children of Israel, who look to other gods and love the raisin cakes of the pagans" (Hosea 3:1 NKJV).*

Their marriage was restored: *"²So I bought her for myself for fifteen shekels of silver, and one and one-half homers of barley. ³And I said to her, "You shall stay with me many days; you shall not play the harlot, nor shall you have a man—so, too will I be toward you" (Hosea 3:2-3 NKJV).* After putting them on the wheel He was then able to restore their marriage. Yes indeed she was adulterous, and giving herself over to her lovers. Yes this was painful for Hosea but he had to look beyond his ache to his healer. Painful in knowing the one he married was out with her lovers, painful in knowing she left her children at home to be with her lovers. Painful in knowing she sought things verses the love he had for her. The Lord had to put her on the wheel, to reshape and mold her again. Her aim was to get things. She did not acknowledge or love anyone but herself. While at the Potter's wheel He begins to strip her of her precious things from her lovers. He stopped all her celebrations. He had to make her over again.

In the midst of his pain Hosea sought the Lord for his healing. Hosea looked beyond the issue behind the ache to His healer. The Lord ordered Hosea to start all over again, to love her. As a child of the King you must learn to seek your healer for He will guide you into all truths. Lord we will cast our burdens on you knowing that you will sustain us. We thank you for not allowing us to be moved, made to slip, fall or fail. We withstand the devil; we are firm in our faith—rooted, established, strong, immovable and determined. Lord thank you that your presence goes with us. We will not fret, nor shall we let our heart be troubled, neither shall we be afraid for our hope is in You, in Jesus name. Amen.

Be determined to stay connected with Jesus. No matter what you face, stay connected to the potter. *"¹⁶ . . . We do not lose heart even though our outward man is perishing, yet the inward man is being renewed day by day. ¹⁷For our light affliction, which is but for a moment, is working for us a far more exceeding and eternal weight of glory, ¹⁸ While we do not look at the things which are seen but at the things which are not seen. For the things which are seen are temporary. But the things which are not seen are eternal" (2 Corinthians 4:16-18, NKJV).*

As Jesus continues the renewal process in you, go forward and remain united to the Lord. Thus, though the outward man may grow old and decay with the years, the inward man continues to grow in grace as long as life lasts. Continue to look beyond your issues to the healer. Spiritual renewal brings new light from God's word, new experiences of grace, cleansing of your heart and mind. Staying in the Potter's hand will bring about a change within you.

"¹⁷ For our light affliction, which is but for a moment, is working for us a far more exceeding and eternal weight of glory" (2 Corinthians 4:17, NKJV). No matter what you are faced with understand and know that it is only a light affliction. It is a condition or problem that produces suffering or pain, it's a light affliction and you will make it. Look beyond your affliction, your condition, your problem, and your pain—to the healer. Why, for our light affliction, is but for a moment? Do you see what is happening within your

affliction? GOD IS WORKING! However, the devil would have you to think that God is no where to be found in the midst of your circumstances. He has you on the wheel. So cast your situation to the Lord and stay on the wheel. *"⁷Casting all your care upon Him, for He cares for you" (1 Peter 5:7, NKJV)*. You must cast it to the Lord for He's able to handle every fiber that pertains to you and your situations.

At this point in your life are you in need of a makeover? What is the spirit of God saying to you? God longs to heal you, He wants to make you whole. Sometimes you may feel like you are fragmented, but despite your feelings God can make you whole. He still loves you. You will be that vessel of honor that is fit for the Master's use. Hold your head up and receive.

INSIGHT AND REVELATION

Hold Your Head Up—*"This is your Make up day"*

Have you allowed your spirit to be clogged up? Are you backed up, congested, blocked, jam packed, overcrowded, packed full of junk? Jesus is ready to do spiritual surgery so that you may be free. Will you allow the glory of the Lord to arise?

Stop waiting for someone else to do things for you. Are you ready to receive your miracle, your blessing, your healing, and your deliverance? It's time for you to receive, are you ready? Then sit at the wheel and allow the Potter to make you over again.

Father we ask that your glory rise upon us, we need your glory to unclog our spirit. *"²For behold, the darkness shall cover the earth, and deep darkness the people; but the Lord will arise over you and his glory will be seen upon you" (Isaiah 60:2 NKJV)*. Arise over us and allow your glory to be seen upon us. Cover us with your glory and presence in Jesus name. Amen.

Insight: The things that the spirit reveals to you at this point are very important to the making of a beautiful vessel. *"¹ Arise and shine for your light has come! And the glory of the Lord is risen upon you" (Isaiah 60:1 NKJV)*.

TALK BACK:
Revelation: In your own words tell what the Lord revealed to you in this chapter.

_____
_____
_____
_____
_____
_____
_____
_____

SECTION IV

MOVING AHEAD IN THE KINGDOM:

This section deals with taking your rightful place.

Chapter 10

Experiencing your Gethsemane

"A place of reality, prayer and surrender"

"[32] Then they came to a place which was named Gethsemane; and He said to His disciples, "Sit here while I pray." [33] And He took Peter, James, and John with Him, and He began to be troubled and deeply distressed. [34] Then He said to them, "My soul is exceedingly sorrowful, even to death. Stay here and watch."[35] He went a little farther, and fell on the ground, and prayed that if it were possible, the hour might pass from Him. [36] And He said, "Abba, Father, all things are possible for You. Take this cup away from Me; nevertheless, not what I will, but what You will."[37] Then He came and found them sleeping, and said to Peter, "Simon, are you sleeping? Could you not watch one hour? [38] Watch and pray, lest you enter into temptation. The spirit indeed is willing, but the flesh is weak."[39] Again He went away and prayed, and spoke the same words. [40] And when He returned, He found them asleep again, for their eyes were heavy; and they did not know what to answer Him. [41] Then He came the third time and said to them, "Are you still sleeping and resting? It is enough! The hour has come; behold, the Son of Man is being betrayed into the hands of sinners. [42] Rise, let us be going. See, My betrayer is at hand" (Mark 14:32-42, NKJV).

Gethsemane was a place of reality, prayer and surrender for Jesus. It was also the place of warning, betrayal and arrest. The experience in Gethsemane was one of strength and power. It was here that Jesus was positioned to ungird the task at hand; He was being prepared for the cross. But even in being prepared it does not neglect the fact that at this point in Jesus life He was troubled and deeply distressed. Even in the midst of being troubled, stirred, afflicted with discomfort and being in need of immediate assistance, Jesus had to position himself for what was to come. When life begins to unfold and more is required of you, you need to find a place of prayer and get in the presence of God. You need to prepare to position yourself for what is coming.

As you experience your Gethsemane get in position. Your Gethsemane is not preparing you to die on the cross but whatever it may be, get in position. Do not fail to prepare. This is your place of change; this is the place where you meet God in prayer about the things that are yet to come (that has been predestined).

Prior to his death, Jesus came to the garden to meet his father. *He said, "My soul is exceedingly sorrowful, even to death."* Jesus knew what He was about to experience within Himself, and knowing the things to come His soul was exceedingly sorrowful, in mental anguish and pain. However, at this point in His life, Jesus decided to go a little further and began to pray. He knew the power of God, He knew what God was able to do, He knew that all things were possible with God. He did not allow his situation to cause Him to run away from the Father, but instead He sought out God's help. How often do you allow your circumstances and situations to move you away from the presence of God? In looking at Jesus' experience, it pushed Him into the presence of God. It was here that He began to pray to the Father. He was well aware of the power of God and therefore asked Him, *"Take this cup away from me; nevertheless, not what I will, but what you will."* Despite how painful this may have been for Jesus, He had to allow God's will to be done in His life. He could not stop the will of His father, for it was predestined for his life.

Even though He wanted the cup to be taken away He came into agreement of letting God's will be done. Do you desire for Jesus to take your cup away? Whatever your answer may be you have to come into agreement of letting God's will be done in your life. Despite how painful or difficult it may be to hold on to your cup of pain and affliction, it is imperative that God's will be done.

What is this cup? For Jesus it was death at the cross. For you and I the cup may be sickness, affliction, disease, bitterness, rejection, drugs, shame, guilt, or pain. It does not matter what is in your cup, what matters is how you handle what's in your cup? How shall you contend with your cup? When will you come into agreement with letting God's will be done in your life concerning your cup? With your cup of affliction God is making something beautiful. He will create a beautiful vessel from your cup, will you surrender; release your cup of affliction? God is making you into a beautiful vessel of honor.

You see Gethsemane was a place of reality, prayer, and surrender for Jesus. It was at Gethsemane where He had to acknowledge what was going on in His life, despite the pain and difficulty. He then went to God in prayer telling Him what was on His heart and how He was feeling. He prayed for God's will to be done concerning his situation, it was then that He was able to surrender His will to the Father.

As you experience your Gethsemane, your place of reality, prayer and surrender what is it that you need to come into reality of? What is going on in your life where you must acknowledge it despite the pain, emptiness and loneliness? Go to God in prayer and tell Him what's on your heart. Tell Him how you feel, pray His word over your feelings, and the situation. Will you surrender your will unto Him? This is your day to experience your Gethsemane, your place of freedom.

Prayer:
> Lord I give myself to you. I surrender my will unto you. I give you all my strengths and weaknesses, vices and virtues, hopes and fears, successes and failures, faith and doubts. I trust that all things will work together for my good. I am called according to your purpose. I receive your mercy, grace, and love into my life. In the name of Jesus, I am now willing to place my body, my soul, my spirit, and my entire life into your hands. I ask that you place me into your perfect will and plan for my life. I place my life completely and unreservedly in your hands, and trust that you will not let anything happen to me outside of your will for me. Father, from this moment on,

I will choose to stay fully surrendered to you all the days of my life, and will allow you to lead and direct my life in the direction that you want it to go. I ask these things in the name and the power and the authority of Jesus Christ, my Savior and friend. Amen.

Gethsemane was also a place of warning, betrayal, and arrest. After praying Jesus would **return to the place where He left his disciples and each time He found them sleeping.** They were not in prayer for what Jesus was about to experience, but even so, he took the time to warn His disciples, addressing Peter, *³⁸ Watch and pray lest you enter into temptation. The spirit indeed is willing but the flesh is weak.*

With the three disciples present at this time, why did Jesus directly address Peter? He knew the plot that Satan had for Peter; He knew how Satan desired to sift him as wheat, as if there was nothing good in him. But he prayed for Peter that his faith failed not. He wanted Peter to be alert for the devil was seeking to devour him. The devil is cunning, he is clever and knows how to tempt you so open your eyes, be watchful of the devil's schemes, and plans; be alert of his devices. Pray and seek God's face. It is time to wake up!

INSIGHT AND REVELATION

Experiencing Your Gethsemane—*"A place of reality, prayer, and surrender"*

"²⁷ Behold, I am the Lord, the God of all flesh. Is there anything too hard for me" (Jeremiah 32:27, NKJV)? Do not give up when facing what may seem impossible, *"²⁶ . . . With God all things are possible"* (Matthew 19:26, NKJV). So despite your place of Gethsemane, you need to know that *"⁴ . . . He who is in you is greater than he who is in the world"* (1 John 4:4, NKJV). God is greater than your place of Gethsemane and he wants you to surrender your will unto him.

There is no deficiency in His power. You must believe that He can do what needs to be done in your life. Expect Him to answer, and then watch for Him to do it. He may work in totally unexpected ways, but He will work with supernatural power. At this very moment, He is looking for people through whom He can demonstrate that power. Why not let it be you? Allow God to give life to those dead things in your life, allow Him to call it into existence. God is calling life to be formed now! He is calling things to come into order now! He is calling forth those things which do not exist as though they did. El Shaddai is God Almighty, the God who can do anything, He is almighty, all-powerful. *"¹⁷ . . . God, who gives life to the dead and calls those things which do not exist as though they did"* (Romans 4:17 NKJV).

Insight: The things that the spirit reveals to you at this point are very important to the making of a beautiful vessel. *"² . . . The LORD is with you while you are with Him. If you seek Him, He will be found by you; but if you forsake Him, He will forsake you" (2 Chronicles 15:2, NKJV).* While at your place of Gethsemane will you take time to seek the Lord? As you do he will be found by you.

TALK BACK:
Revelation: In your own words tell what the Lord revealed to you in this chapter.

Chapter 11

Trouble and the Open Door

"The Battle in Between"

In every season of trouble an open door is near. Satan will do all he can to make you see only the trouble while bypassing your open door. There is a battle going on between your trouble and your open door. Understand and know that yes there may be trouble but there is still an open door. What are you allowing to happen during the in between times of your battle, struggle, and your open door? Let us examine the children of Israel during their time of struggle and open door. What were they doing in their in between time? What did they accomplish? What did they gain during their in between time?

Leaving Egypt: *"¹⁸So God led the people around by way of the wilderness of the Red Sea. And the children of Israel went up in orderly ranks out of the land of Egypt. ²¹ And the Lord went before them by day in a pillar of cloud to lead the way, and by night in a pillar of fire to give them light, so as to go by day and night" (Exodus 13:18, 21 NKJV).* Here we witness how the children of Israel left the land of Egypt and how the Lord led them by day and night through out the journey.

"¹ Now the Lord spoke to Moses, saying. ²Speak to the children of Israel, that they turn and camp BEFORE Pitlahiroth, between Migdol and the seas, opposite the Baal Aephon; you shall camp before it by the sea. ³ For Pharaoh will say of the children of Israel, they are bewildered by the land; the wilderness has closed them in.' ⁴ Then I will harden Pharaoh's heart, so that he will pursue them; and I will gain honor over Pharaoh and over all his army, that the Egyptians may know that I am the Lord." And they did so" (Exodus 14:1, 2, 4 NKJV). Once again we see the Lord giving the people instruction. He tells them to camp by the sea. He tells them the plans for the next move and how He will harden Pharaoh's heart so He will indeed pursue them but as He does He will gain honor over him and all his army. The Lord told Moses ahead of time what was going to happen so surely they could see their open door in the midst of their trouble which was about to transpire.

The Trouble: *"⁵ Now it was told the king of Egypt that the people had fled, and the heart of Pharaoh and his servants was turned against the people; and they said, "Why have we done this, that we have let Israel go from serving us?" ⁶ So he made ready his chariot and took his people with him. ⁷ Also, he took six hundred choice chariots, and all the chariots of Egypt with captains over every one of them. ⁸ And the LORD hardened the heart of Pharaoh king of Egypt, and he pursued the children of Israel; and the children of Israel went out with boldness. ⁹ So the Egyptians pursued them, all the horses and chariots of Pharaoh, his horsemen and his army, and overtook them camping by the sea beside Pi Hahiroth, before Baal Zephon" (Exodus 14:5-9, NKJV).* Here we see how indeed the things spoken by the Lord happened just as He said. Pharaoh and his army began to pursue the children of Israel and they went out with boldness. He took his great and mighty army with him in an attempt to detain, the children of Israel. Pharaoh felt he had the manpower to detain them. The trouble began to unravel as they approached the children of Israel. You must know that no matter how much trouble you face, God is greater than any trouble and an open door is near thee.

In Between Time: *"¹¹ Then they said to Moses, "Because there were no graves in Egypt, have you taken us away to die in the wilderness? Why have you so dealt with us, to bring us up out of Egypt? ¹² Is this not the word that we told you in Egypt, saying, 'Let us alone that we may serve the Egyptians'? For it would have been better for us to serve the Egyptians than that we should die in the wilderness."¹³ And Moses said to the people, "Do not be afraid. Stand still, and see the salvation of the Lord, which He will accomplish for you today. For the Egyptians whom you see today, you shall see again no more forever. ¹⁴ The Lord will fight for you, and you shall hold your peace." ¹⁵ And the Lord said to Moses, "Why do you cry to Me? Tell the children of Israel to go forward" (Exodus 14:11-15, NKJV).*

As trouble drew near the children of Israel were afraid and began to cry out to the Lord. Did they forget what the Lord spoke previously about the plan to harden Pharaoh's heart which would cause Him to pursue them? Had they forgotten when they saw his army approaching them? Because the pressure was on, they could only see the trap laid out before them. Wilderness land on the left, wilderness land on the right and a great sea in front of them. What were they to do now? They asked, "Why did He bring them to this place to die, they could have stayed in Egypt?" They could have endured the rough treatment in Egypt; after all they became accustomed to the treatment. Do you see how when trouble comes, and it looks like there is no way out; how one can allow their mouth to speak death? How about you, what do you speak during the in between times of your trouble, struggle, and seeking your open door?

What I love is the Lord's response in the midst of their trouble, whining, and complaining. He said, *"Why do you cry to Me? Tell the children of Israel to go forward."* Yes, trouble is behind you but I am in charge here, I have already made a way, so stop crying and go forward! In order for the children of Israel to go through their open door they had to move forward, they could not remain in that place, crying, whining, and complaining. They had to do something and so do you. You will never reach your open door by always remaining in the same place and saying the same things over and over again. Like the Lord told the children of Israel, *"Why do you cry to Me? (Insert your name) go forward."* Stop whining and complaining about the same things year after year after year, get up and move forward. If **you** want to reach your open door **you** have got to get up from where you are and do something. Go forward!

Open Door: *"¹⁶ But lift up your rod, and stretch out your hand over the sea and divide it. And the children of Israel shall go on dry ground through the midst of the sea. ¹⁷ And I indeed will harden the hearts of the Egyptians, and they shall follow them. So I will gain honor over Pharaoh and over all his army, his chariots, and his horsemen. ¹⁸ Then the Egyptians shall know that I am the Lord, when I have gained honor for Myself over Pharaoh, his chariots, and his horsemen." ²¹ Then Moses stretched out his hand over the sea; and the LORD caused the sea to go back by a strong east wind all that night,* *and made the sea into dry land, and the waters were divided. ²² So the children of Israel went into the midst of the sea on the dry ground, and the waters were a wall to them on their right hand and on their left. ²³ And the Egyptians pursued and went after them into the midst of the sea, all Pharaoh's horses, his chariots, and his horsemen.²⁴ Now it came to pass, in the morning watch, that the LORD looked down upon the army of the Egyptians through the pillar of fire and cloud, and He troubled the army of the Egyptians. ²⁵ And He took off their chariot wheels, so that they drove them with difficulty; and the Egyptians said, "Let us flee from the face of Israel, for the LORD fights for them against the Egyptians."²⁶ Then the LORD said to Moses, "Stretch out your hand over the sea, that the waters may come back upon the Egyptians, on their chariots, and on their horsemen." ²⁷ And Moses stretched out his hand over the sea; and when the morning appeared, the sea returned to its full depth, while the Egyptians were fleeing into it. So the LORD overthrew the Egyptians in the midst of the sea. ²⁸ Then the waters returned and covered the chariots, the horsemen, and all the army of Pharaoh that came into the sea after them. Not so much as one of them remained. ²⁹ But the children of Israel had walked on dry land in the midst of the sea, and the waters were a wall to them on their right hand and on their left" (Exodus 14:16-29, NKJV).* Once again the Lord gives the children of Israel instructions; He made a way so they could walk on dry ground through the midst of the Red Sea. The enemy of course kept pursuing them and the Lord fought for them. He overthrew the Egyptians in the midst of the Sea. The waters turned and covered the strong man's army and all his horses and chariots went in the sea after them.

Even though they were faced with trouble, at the rear there was an open door. During their in between time the children of Israel were found whining and complaining, they did nothing constructive. They did not see any good in what they were going through. During your times of struggle, battle, and trouble what are you doing? How do you respond in your in between times? How does it benefit you? Remember your open door is near. In order for the children of Israel to be free, they had to move forward. They had to leave their familiar place; they had to do something in order to cross over to the other side. So in order for you to go through your open door you need to do something. God has been dealing with you about your situation and now it is time for you to do something. You must first accept what He is saying then you have to move forward in the things He has been dealing with you about. I don't know what God has been speaking to you to move forward in but I do know you need to make a move! Sons and daughters of the King do something, get up and make a move! For we serve a God who has the power to open a way through obstacles, power to open a way through your lack, power to open a way through your circumstance. It's your time to cross over.

- It's time for you to leave that destructive relationship.
- It's time for you to let go of those bad habits.
- It's time for you to be delivered and set free.
- It's time for you to leave the familiar and step out into something new.
- It's time for you to come to that new place in the Spirit realm; there is an open door for you.

INSIGHT AND REVELATION

Trouble and the Open Door—*"The Battle in Between"*

The door of freedom can be opened in the worst of problems. Stop allowing the devil to blind you by your troubles till you can not view your open door that is before you. **There is an open door for you**. During your in between time learn to give God praise. He was able to cause water in the Red Sea to make a wall on the left and right leaving dry ground for the children of Israel to pass through, how much more can He do for you? He is a great God and let's give Him praise now. *"30 The children of Israel saw all that God has done" (Exodus 14:30, NKJV).*

Insight: The things that the spirit reveals to you at this point are very important to the making of a beautiful vessel. *"8 I have set before you an open door and no one can shut it" (Revelation 3:8, NKJV).* When God sets before you an open door don't worry about anyone trying to shut it.

TALK BACK:
Revelation: In your own words tell what the Lord revealed to you in this chapter.

Chapter 12

The Plan

"He's Calling You Forth"

"⁵ Before I formed you in the womb I knew you, before you were born I set you apart; I appointed you as a prophet to the nations. ⁶ Ah Sovereign Lord, I said, "I do not know how to speak; I am only a child." ⁷But the Lord said to me, "Do not say, 'I am only a child.' You must go to everyone I send you to and say whatever I command you. ⁸ Do not be afraid of them, for I am with you and will rescue you," declares the Lord" (Jeremiah 1:5-8, NIV).

God had a plan for Jeremiah's life and he called him forth. He now has a plan for your life and he's calling you forth. He told Jeremiah, **"Before I formed you in the womb I knew you."** Before there was a Jeremiah, God knew him. Before there was (insert your name), God knew you. You must understand that before you were created, made or came into existence, Christ knew you. He was already familiar with you; he already knew what he designed for you to be.

Because of the great plan He has for your life He had to set you apart before you were born. Despite all that you have been through He knew you. Therefore, He knew that you would be able to complete what He has called for you to do.

He appointed Jeremiah to be a prophet to the nations, someone to speak God's message to the people. Just like He called Jeremiah forth to be a prophet, He will likewise call you forth for what He has for you. There is a plan and because He has a plan He will set you apart for that which He calls you to do. What He designed you for, He will call you forth. When one is called forth, they must arise to the occasion at hand. They must leave the familiar and go where He is calling them to. For instance, He created Jeremiah then He called him forth for what He designed for him to do (Prophet). He created Noah, then He called him forth for what He designed for him to do as well (Build the ark). It does not matter what has transpired in your life, all you have to do when He calls you forth is to walk in it. For whatever He calls you to, He will bring you through. Whatever He designed you for, He will call you forth. He will not call anyone forth before their time because God does not operate like that.

He did not call Daniel forth to do what He called Moses to do. In like manner, when He calls you forth then you have to know it's the call for you. He is well aware of who He is calling for a particular mission, so think it not strange for the call that He has for your life. For some, God has already called them forth, but because of limited thinking they refuse to heed the call. When Jonah was called forth for a task He went in the opposite direction and as a result He ended up in the belly of a fish, simply because He refused to heed the call. I speak to your heart on today, don't refuse the call. Go forth when He calls you. He will show you how to develop your gifts, equipping you with what you need to become that vessel fit for the Master's use.

Sometimes in life you may think you are not fit for the call. The enemy will feed your thoughts to go against all that Christ has called you to. He will even try to make you fit in where you don't belong. God is aware of whom He has created you to be. But because of your doubts and disbelief you ask God?

WHO AM I?

What's my name?
Why am I a square?
Who said I was supposed to stand out in the crowd, at church, at work and around my family?
I want to be included with them, the in crowd.
Why do I have to be different?
All of my life I could feel it; I want to be like others, but the inner me keeps popping up showing me my true self.
I then go and try to dress differently, talk differently but it doesn't feel right.
It seems as if so many people can do a better job, with taking care of their bodies, their kids and their homes.
But I can't seem to find the real me?
Do others see that thing that I desperately try to hide?
That thing that I do, that has the ability to draw some and repel others?
Don't hate me I just want to be like you!
Who am I?
Can you tell me?
Everyone knows but me, puzzled, lonely and confused.
(Submitted by a friend, 6/9/2005)

You are accepted by God, you are God's child and he loves you with an everlasting love. You have been redeemed and forgiven of all your sins. You are complete in Christ. You have been chosen and appointed by God to bear fruit. You are his crafted workmanship, created to do good works. You are a vessel of treasure and because God arms you with strength you can do all things. It's time to stop living out of who people say you are and who you think you are, instead take hold of the truth of God's word and be who he said that you are.

Don't forget, YOU are a Kings kid and he has great things for you. Wealth and riches are in your house. You have been hidden in Christ and you have the mind of Christ, you have been given the ability to speak into the atmosphere and change things. He has empowered you with wisdom and the gates of opportunity are open for you. You will walk in all that God has for you. That is who you are!

So all that God has designed you for, He is now calling you forth, the real you to come forth. His purposes cannot be stopped. One may hinder the call but it will not stop the call. If He has designed you for it, He will call you forth. Look what happens when He calls you forth: ***"Ah Sovereign Lord," Jeremiah said, "I do not know how to speak; I am only a child."*** Jeremiah immediately made an excuse for the call on his life. He began to compare himself against how he felt a "Prophet" was to speak. He said, I cannot speak finely or word things right as a messenger from God, for I am only a child. He felt he could not speak with authority and people would listen. God sees what He has already put on the inside of you. You are capable of doing what He has called you to do. Do not allow how you see yourself to hinder the call for your life. Self perception is not always the correct perception.

One may even object the call on their life, but even so there is still a call. When Jonah objected God's call for his life, he ended up in the belly of a fish for three days. Who knows where you will end up if you object to God's call? When someone is in court and they say, "I object your honor," we understand that they are not in agreement with what is being said. You may have conflict with your call and object, but God is well aware of the call on your life. He knows what you have been designed for, stop objecting and go forth! Even Jeremiah tried to object by saying "I do not know how to speak, I'm only a child." What are your objections/excuses?

I OBJECT LORD

- I don't know enough.
- I'm not quite ready.
- What will I say?
- Use someone else.

He may be calling you forth to make a difference in the area of your attitude and behavior, but you keep objecting and making excuses for your bad attitude and ugly behavior. It is time to take a look at yourself and stop blaming others. It's you and He is calling you forth to allow His image to shine through you. He is calling you forth to change.

God specializes in using imperfect people and things that are broken. Even with Jeremiah, it was not about his educational level, it was about what God formed in him. Jeremiah was afraid of his call, but he was still called forth. Do you find yourself afraid of the call, even so, the call is still there and you must go forth! You must learn to be you and do what He has called you to.

The Lord said to Jeremiah, "Do not say, 'I am only a child.' You must go to everyone I send you to and say whatever I command you. The Lord said to Jeremiah, there will be NO BUTS, NO OBJECTIONS, and NO EXCUSES. The words "must go" carry the meaning that it is an absolute requirement. And you must say whatever God commands, follow his direct orders. SPEAK it as it should be spoken. It was a must, a requirement for Jeremiah to go and say all that the Lord instructed him to stay. In your life you must follow instructions as well. Do not allow your weakness to make you draw back from what God is calling you to! Even though Jeremiah was young, the Lord equipped him to go to all to whom He sent him to.

Do not be afraid of them, for I am with you and will rescue you," declares the Lord. Do not reject those who may cause you trouble—The Lord will protect you. Do not be afraid of their faces—even though they look big and try to scare you, trying to make you back down—The Lord is with you. Do not be afraid to speak even though they look angry—The Lord is there so deliver your message with power and authority. Do what you've been called, designed to do BE BOLD! God is with you to rescue you; he goes along with those whom he sends.

So do not object the call, He will equip you to do what you've been fitted to do. If He calls you to speak a word before the people, He will make a way for you to speak that word with clarity and understanding. You have already been fitted for what He has designed for you and it's a perfect fit. Like a wedding dress or a suit, you make sure it fits the person making the purchase, and so it is the same with ministry. You've been fitted for it! God has formed you for it. Now go forth for what He is calling you to.

He knows the plan for your life.

INSIGHT AND REVELATION

THE PLAN—*"He's Calling You Forth"*

The Plan: I often find myself kicking against the Lord's plan for my life. But I notice the harder I kick the higher I get in Him. As I try to travel on "my road" that I have drawn up for my life, the more difficult my journey becomes. Every time I try to travel on my road I find myself running into a detour. It's like I find myself at a halt and I'm unable to move forward, unable to keep traveling on my road. You see "my road" is a comfortable place that I've made for myself. It's where I prefer to be. But then the Lord kindly directs me to the nearest stop. He realizes that I am empty, my fuel is out, and a refilling needs to take place.

So while I'm at this place He tells me that my parts need to be cleaned. He then begins to empty out my mess, my thoughts, my ways, my plans, my direction, and thoroughly cleanses me from within.

After the cleaning He begins to give directions for my life. He allows me to be refilled with his presence, and with his anointing. As I pull away, leaving that place, I feel refreshed, revived, and restored because I have been made anew. I have been cleansed.

But during the course of my days, and months, I often find myself going back to the same patterns of thinking. I find myself feeding my flesh what it wants. Once again I'm on my road, and I find myself headed for a detour all over again.

Nevertheless, Jesus gently reminds me about the plans He has for my life. How I can do good works through Him and how the path for my life, I will travel with ease while abiding in Him. He kindly reminds me to forget the past for it does not matter where you have been. What matters the most is what are you going to do from this point forward?

Now at this point in my life I'm able to bear more, to do more, and be at ease about it. Why, because I've come to realize this important truth that it's Christ working on the inside of me, supporting me, lifting me up and pushing me to my destiny in Him. Therefore, I am now able to work towards the plans that He has for my life.

So inspite of the stops and many detours along the way I'm still well able to do that in which He has given me to do. How about you, whose plans are you following? Which road have you taken? Is it in His Plans? *"For I know the plans I have for you," declares the Lord, "plans to prosper you and not to harm, plans to give you a hope and a future. Then you will call upon and come and pray to me, and I will listen to you. You will seek me and find me when you seek me with all your heart" (Jeremiah 29:11-13, NIV).*

Insight: The things that the spirit reveals to you at this point are very important to the making of a beautiful vessel. *"¹⁷ And whatever you do in word or deed, do all in the name of the Lord Jesus, giving thanks to God and the Father by him" (Colossians 3:17, NKJV).*

TALK BACK:
Revelation: In your own words tell what the Lord revealed to you in this chapter.

_____
_____
_____
_____
_____
_____
_____
_____
_____
_____
_____
_____
_____
_____
_____
_____
_____
_____

Chapter 13

Putting it all Together and Moving Ahead

It's time to pick up the pieces of your life and move ahead, you've got to keep building. After everything you have experienced, endured, and encountered the Lord wants you to pick up the pieces, put it all together and move ahead. No longer will you be held captive by your struggle, loss, and pain. He is calling for order in the midst of it all.

Moses led the children of Israel out of Egypt and as time continued he had to release leadership of the Israelites. Moses had to pass it on to the next generation. God put things together so the children of Israel could continue to move straight ahead. In your life God is putting things in order so you can continue to move ahead. This is your time to move ahead, therefore, it is imperative that you keep building upon that in which Christ has given you. God is putting things together so the blessings can flow continuously from generation to generation. There shall no longer be a gap between the different generations. God has prepared someone to take the next step and move ahead.

Because God is putting it all together the previous generation will supply the next generation with what they need to move ahead. *"¹ Moses went out and spoke these words to all Israel: ² I am now a hundred and twenty years old and I am no longer able to lead you. ⁷ Then Moses called Joshua and said to him in the sight of all Israel, "Be strong and of good courage, for you must go with this people to the land which the LORD has sworn to their fathers to give them, and you shall cause them to inherit it. ⁸ And the LORD, He is the One who goes before you. He will be with you, He will not leave you nor forsake you; do not fear nor be dismayed" (Deuteronomy 31:1-2, 7-8, NIV).*

We witnessed how the Lord allowed Moses to prepare Israel for the next move of God, utilizing their new successor Joshua. Moses had to pass the knowledge and blessings on to the next generation. He encouraged Joshua's heart for the call. It was now time for Joshua to get up and move forward. *"²³ The LORD gave this command to Joshua son of Nun: "Be strong and courageous, for you will bring the Israelites into the land I promised them on oath, and I myself will be with you" (Deuteronomy 31:23 NIV).* The Lord encouraged Joshua and gave him instructions for leading the people. The Lord was pulling it all together prior to Moses' death. He was not going to leave the people empty handed and He will not leave you empty handed. He's pulling it all together for you right now.

He has given you the plan for your life and has created you into a beautiful vessel. He has blessed you to be able to achieve what He has called you to do. Now be strong and courageous, walk in His authority, and do it. He said, "I will be with you," therefore you have no excuse. You must walk towards the things He is calling you to. Put it all together and move ahead. No longer wrestle or struggle with what you think is right, but go ahead and move forward in your ministry, in serving Christ, and in your worship. It's time to move ahead in doing kingdom work.

Passing the blessings on to the next generation: As sons and daughters of the King are you passing the blessings on to the next generation? You have an obligation to pass it down to multiple generations. You do not have the right to stop the blessings from flowing from one generation to the next. In the picture below we see four different generations and each generation is passing the blessings to the next generation. Then when you get to the fourth generation there should be multiple blessings at his feet. He will have mountain of opportunities in life, he can be whatever he wants to be. On the side you see the soldier who is always in the army of the Lord. As a family being in God's army the blessings, promises are yes and amen. The opportunities are great. You can receive multiple blessings being passed to you from multiple places but the one receiving the blessings must know and understand what to do with the blessing. Do not waste your blessings on prodigal living. Stay in God's army of life and he will train, teach, guide, and instruct you concerning your blessings, for you have been predestined for purpose.

Since you are predestined for purpose, you like Moses must pass the blessing on to the next generation. Receive instructions and move forward:

After Moses death, the Lord commanded Joshua to move ahead *"¹ After the death of Moses the servant of the LORD the LORD said to Joshua son of Nun, Moses' aide: ² " Moses my servant is dead. Now then, you and all these people, get ready to cross the Jordan River into the land I am about to give to them—to the Israelites. ⁵ No one will be able to stand against you all the days of your life. As I was with Moses, so I will be with you; I will never leave you nor forsake you. ⁶ Be strong and courageous, because you will lead these people to inherit the land I swore to their ancestors to give them. ⁷ "Be strong and very courageous. Be careful to obey all the law my servant Moses gave you; do not turn from it to the right or to the left, that you may be successful wherever you go. ⁸ Keep this Book of the Law always on your lips; meditate on it day and night, so that you may be careful to do everything written in it. Then you will be prosperous and successful. ⁹ Have I not commanded you? Be strong and courageous. Do not be afraid; do not be discouraged, for the LORD your God will be with you wherever you go" (Joshua 1:1-2, 5-9 NIV).*

He told Joshua and the people to get ready to cross the Jordan. Your next place in life is a transitional place; it's a place of crossing over. As you finish this chapter you need to get ready to cross your next place in life. What is God calling you towards? What has he prepared you for? As He was with Moses and Joshua, He will also be with you. He said, *"⁵ I will never leave you nor forsake you" (Joshua 1:5, NIV)*. I don't care what you have heard, the Lord has promised to never leave you nor forsake you.

You must obey the word so you can be successful everywhere you go. *"⁸ Keep this Book of the Law always on your lips; meditate on it day and night, so that you may be careful to do everything written in it. Then you will be prosperous and successful" (Joshua 1:8, NIV)*. He gave Joshua instructions on how to move the people forward and how to be prosperous and successful at the same time. If you desire to be prosperous and successful then **fully obey** the **word of God**.

He told Joshua, *"⁹ Do not be terrified; do not be discouraged, for I will be with you where ever you go" (Joshua 1:9, NIV)*. Joshua had the promise and so do you. Do not fret or be anxious for the Lord has promised to be with you.

Now as you seek to put the pieces of your life together you must *"⁶ Humble yourselves, therefore, under God's mighty hand, that he may lift you up in due time. ⁷ Cast all your anxiety on him because he cares for you. ⁸ Be self-controlled and alert. Your enemy the devil prowls around like a roaring lion looking for someone to devour. ⁹Resist him, standing firm in the Faith" (1 Peter 5:6-9 NIV)*. Submit yourselves under God's mighty hand. Stop murmuring against Him; be still under the rod, and under your circumstances. Despise not the chastening of the Lord; He has your best interest at heart. To be under His hands in a humble manner is safe and profitable.

"⁵ For in the time of trouble He shall hide me in his pavilion, in the secret place of His tabernacle He shall hide me. He shall set me high upon a rock" (Psalm 27:5 NKJV). When

you are hidden then trouble can't get to you. The devil can't get to you, you will leave him confused and puzzled. Putting ourselves under God's mighty hand and care is the way to exaltation. He shall exalt the humble; and lift them up in due time. You can make it! Your time is coming! So therefore *"Cast all your anxiety on him because he cares for you."*

[1]**Anxiety:** distress about future circumstances, a troubled state of mind, uneasiness, worry.

You must cast what pulls you apart unto the Lord. Release it, and let it go. There is no need for you to worry or be in distress about your future circumstances. Give it to the Lord because He cares for you. He does not want you to have a troubled mind or be in a state of uneasiness. Instead cast it to Him, if it's pulling you apart throw it to Him!

For example, Jesus wants you here in the middle doing XYZ, but because of your pending circumstances you feel you can't do XYZ, and it's pulling you away from where Jesus wants you to be. Instead of giving into the pressure, the tug that is trying to pull you apart from Jesus—cast it on Him knowing that He will bring it all together for the purpose of moving ahead.

"Be self-controlled and alert. Your enemy the devil prowls around like a roaring lion looking for someone to devour." You must be alert to the pitfalls of your surroundings. Make certain that you do not give in to the devil to those pending circumstances. The devil prowls around like a roaring lion looking for someone to devour. He is cunning and cruel; he attacks when least expected and seeks to destroy all in whom he attacks. You better take a stand and tell the devil "It won't be me!" Resist him, oppose with force, remain firm in opposing him, refrain from giving in to him. No matter what you're facing don't give in. Stand firm and fight rather than flee.

Victory comes when we remain committed to the Lord because he is greater than our enemy. So instead of allowing the enemies, pending circumstances to pull you out of God's will for your life, learn to fight and remain committed to the Lord. If it's pulling you apart don't allow it to settle in your heart, instead, cast, and throw it upon the Lord. Often times we allow things in our heart to settle in causing us to be inactive, idle, and often ineffective in one way or another. Our heart is God's ground; it's the preparation place. It's the place where we can produce a harvest of work, whether good or bad. You must release the situation that you have allowed to settle in your heart.

Prayer:
>Put your hand on your heart and begin to talk to the Lord, tell Him what you desire to take place this day. Lord I release the issues of my heart unto you, for they are pulling me apart. Lord I need you to remove (_____) from my heart. I seek to do your will. I seek to be in your presence and I need you to deal with the issues of my heart. I'm ready to move ahead in you. So I release the pressure of trying to fit where I don't belong. Every idle thing that lurks in my heart remove it from me so I can be a better person, spouse, friend, co worker, mother, daughter,

son, father, and brother. I give it to you right now; take control over me, over the issues of my heart. I cast it upon you, in Jesus name. Amen.

INSIGHT AND REVELATION

Putting it all Together and Moving Ahead

"¹ Let us lay aside every weight, and the sin which so easily ensnares us, and let us run with endurance the race that is set before us, ² looking unto Jesus, the author and finisher of our faith" (Hebrews 12:1-2, NKJV). It's time to run with endurance the race that has been set before you. In life one may find they are running away from the things of God. Running in circles only to find they are not advancing. Are you tired of running in circles? Then lay aside every weight, every hindrance, and every sin which ensnares or traps you. Now run towards your King, run towards Jesus Christ. Run with endurance. The race has been set. Which direction will you run? How will you contend with the issues (sin) in your life? Will you keep running in the opposite direction, carrying your weight or will you lay your weight aside and run towards your King with endurance?

In life everyone has things that they must deal with; a decision has to be made. Your decision has the potential to affect your life. It could hinder your ability to be creative or productive. It could open doors and avenues for you to walk into your destiny. How will you handle your issues?

After reading this book my prayer is that you will continue to allow the Spirit of God to minister to you. Before you were formed in the womb He had a plan for your life. God has great plans for you, but you must choose to seek Him for the plans. You have to decide to grow in your relationship with God. Let us stop surviving and learn to live in Christ. Are you ready to walk in God's plan for your life? Then lay aside the weight, issue, sin, laziness, cursing and run with endurance the race that is set before you. Despite what has happened, you need to run! Despite the odds and challenges, run!

Prayer:
By faith, Lord I will put off the old self, old habits, and put on the new self, put on Christ. I stand in victory because Christ will help me to live above sin. I choose to put off the old nature with its selfishness, pride, fear and corruption. I put on the new nature of love, courage, and strength. I claim my place in Christ to be victorious with Him over all the enemies of my soul. Holy Sprit fill me, come into my life, and cast out every foe operating against me. In the name of Jesus, I completely surrender myself to you. I choose not to be conformed to this world. I choose to be transformed by the renewing of my mind, and I pray that you will show me your will and enable me to walk **in all** the fullness of your will for the rest of my days on earth. In Jesus Name. Amen.

Insight: The things that the spirit reveals to you at this point are very important to the making of a beautiful vessel. *"¹⁸Assuredly, I say to you, whatever you bind on earth will* *be bound in heaven, and whatever you loose on earth will be loosed in heaven" (Matthew 18:18, NKJV).*

TALK BACK:
Revelation: In your own words tell what the Lord revealed to you in this chapter.

Taking another Look at Your Life

"27 So God created man in His own image; in the image of God He created him; male and female He created them. 28 Then God blessed them, and God said to them, "Be fruitful and multiply; fill the earth and subdue it; have dominion over the fish of the sea, over the birds of the air, and over every living thing that moves on the earth" (Genesis 1:27-28, NKJV).

God created you in his image and likeness, so built within you is the ability to create and to be fruitful. How will you use your abilities to cause an increase upon the earth? Take dominion and walk in your God given authority. God has given you potential. This is the capability of being but not yet in existence. You have an unlimited amount of potential in Christ. He operates without limits. You may proceed and go forth without restrictions, it's time to operate within the limits of God's power = unlimited potential. Stop allowing your past to hinder your future. You are equipped with adequate power to perform what God requires of you. You shall operate under the anointing, producing fruit for the Kingdom of God.

Take a moment and examine your life so you can move forward. As you look at where you are standing what do you see? What is your vision? Where are you headed? I encourage you to write your vision and make it plain. If you can't see where you are headed in the future then you will not be prepared.

"2 Then the LORD answered me and said: Write the vision and make it plain on tablets, that he may run who reads it. 3 For the vision is yet for an appointed time; but at the end it will speak, and it will not lie. Though it tarries, wait for it; because it will surely come, it will not tarry"(Habakkuk 2: 2-3, NKJV).

A vision is something that has been seen. How can you run with something you can not see? The above scriptures tells you that it will be a vision for an appointed time but at the end of that time it shall speak, it shall come to pass, it will not lie. The vision will be accomplished in and through you at the appointed time.

Though it tarries, takes a while to be so in your life "wait" for it, it will happen, it will surely come. It will not tarry forever, it's on the way. But you've got to see it.

When I think about the word tarry it carries the meaning that even though it is not before you, it may have been delayed, it may be in a holding place, lingering, but it is coming. It is moving at a certain pace, in your direction. You need to simply believe. In your tarrying state do not allow the enemy an open door to speak into your hearing. Close the door completely on the devil. God has already given somebody a vision and because it has tarried you open your ears to the devil, you allowed him to talk you out of your vision God has given for your life. On today, you are going to take back your vision though it tarries, it will surely come!

You serve a God who does not lie; His word will not return unto Him void, He is a promise keeper. So you can count it as a done deal in Jesus' name. Take back your vision for it is so, it is for you and your household. I speak to your spirit now to get up and believe the vision, wash your thinking, wash your eyes, and wash your mouth with the word of God. Renew now! Prepare now! For your vision is on the way. Can you see it?

God did not tell you to make the vision happen. Your part is to see it, believe it, write it and make it plain. He will bring it to past and it will not only be a blessing to you but to thousands of others as well. So even though it may tarry, remain in a temporarily place, it shall come to pass. Don't stop believing it's on the way!

It's time to make our confession plain:
Lord, I will keep building my life regardless of my circumstances and faults; despite my mishaps and being ridiculed. I will keep building layer by layer upon my foundation. I will be a great representative for Christ. I understand that my foundation is important and I must do something. I will keep building.

I belong to you and I surrender **my will totally and completely** to you. Do what you please in and through me. I avail myself to you. As I make a commitment to submit myself under your mighty hand I will fear no evil, I will be at peace fully operating in your complete will for my life.

I boldly make my confession to the Lord on this day, (Insert exact date) of (Insert the Month), in year of (insert year). Amen!

TALK BACK:
Revelation: In your own words tell what the Lord revealed to you in this chapter.

_____
_____
_____
_____
_____
_____
_____
_____
_____
_____
_____
_____
_____
_____
_____
_____
_____
_____